BFI TV Classics

BFI TV Classics is a series of books celebrating key individual television programmes and series. Television scholars, critics and novelists provide critical readings underpinned with careful research, alongside a personal response to the programme and a case for its 'classic' status.

Editorial Advisory Board:
Stella Bruzzi, *University of Warwick*
Glyn Davis, *Glasgow School of Art*
Mark Duguid, *British Film Institute*
Jason Jacobs, *University of Queensland*
Karen Lury, *University of Glasgow*
Toby Miller, *University of California, Riverside*
Rachel Moseley, *University of Warwick*
Phil Wickham, *University of Exeter*

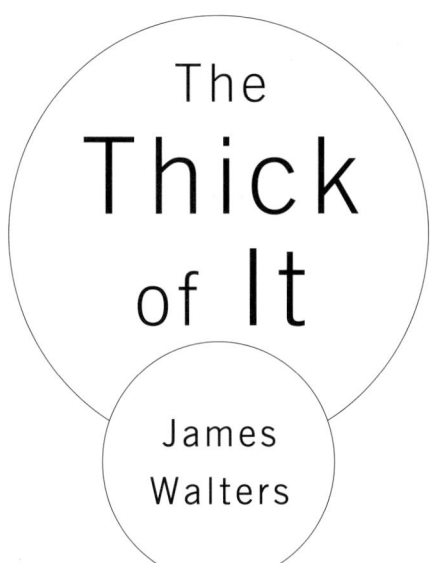

The Thick of It

James Walters

A BFI book published by Palgrave

© James Walters 2016

All rights reserved. No reproduction, copy or transmission of this publication may be made without written permission. No portion of this publication may be reproduced, copied or transmitted save with written permission or in accordance with the provisions of the Copyright, Designs and Patents Act 1988, or under the terms of any licence permitting limited copying issued by the Copyright Licensing Agency, Saffron House, 6–10 Kirby Street, London EC1N 8TS. Any person who does any unauthorised act in relation to this publication may be liable to criminal prosecution and civil claims for damages.

The author has asserted his right to be identified as the author of this work in accordance with the Copyright, Designs and Patents Act 1988.

Images from *The Thick of It*, © BBC; *House of Cards*, © Media Rights Capital, Panic Pictures (II) and Trigger Street Productions; *Friends*, © Warner Bros. Television and Bright/Kauffman/Crane Productions; *The Office*, © BBC; *Yes, Prime Minister*, © BBC; *In the Loop*, © BBC Films, UK Film Council and Aramid Entertainment Fund; *Veep*, © Dundee Productions

Whilst considerable effort has been made to correctly identify the copyright holders, this has not been possible in all cases. We apologise for any omissions or mistakes in the credits and we will endeavour to remedy, in future editions, errors brought to our attention by the relevant rights holder.

None of the content of this publication is intended to imply that it is endorsed by the programme's broadcaster or production companies involved.

First published in 2016 by
PALGRAVE

on behalf of the

BRITISH FILM INSTITUTE
21 Stephen Street, London W1T 1LN
www.bfi.org.uk

There's more to discover about film and television through the BFI. Our world-renowned archive, cinemas, festivals, films, publications and learning resources are here to inspire you.

PALGRAVE in the UK is an imprint of Macmillan Publishers Limited, registered in England, company number 785998, of 4 Crinan Street, London N1 9XW. Palgrave® and Macmillan® are registered trademarks in the United States, the United Kingdom, Europe and other countries.

Set by Integra Software Services Pvt., Pondicherry, India
Printed in China

This book is printed on paper suitable for recycling and made from fully managed and sustained forest sources. Logging, pulping and manufacturing processes are expected to conform to the environmental regulations of the country of origin.

British Library Cataloguing-in-Publication Data
A catalogue record for this book is available from the British Library
A catalog record for this book is available from the Library of Congress

ISBN 978-1-84457-750-7

Contents

Acknowledgements vii
Preface ix

1 Achievement 1
2 Style 25
3 Words 55
4 Spaces 75
5 Adaptation 95

Notes 105
Bibliography 106
Credits 108
Index 127

Acknowledgements

I teach an Aesthetics of Television class at the University of Birmingham and would like to begin by thanking the many students who have joined me over the years to share their valuable ideas about television. I have presented draft sections of this book at the universities of Birmingham, Canterbury Christchurch, Hertfordshire, Kent and Lincoln, and the enthusiastic responses I received at those institutions have helped shape the material for the better. Many friends and colleagues have kindly encouraged the prospect of a book on *The Thick of It*, and I thank them for spurring me on. It says something about the slowness of my writing that I need to thank three consecutive commissioning editors at BFI/Palgrave, Rebecca Barden, Lucinda Knight and Nicola Cattini, for their guidance, support and faith in the project. Finally, I reserve special thanks for Simon Page, whose teaching first introduced me to the study of television. Always funny and often political, Simon has been an inspiration for many years and I dedicate this book to him.

Preface

There are many ways to think and write about television programmes. This book offers a critical analysis of *The Thick of It*, focused on a group of themes that I take to be important. Although I refer to the making of the programme and some of the individuals involved, I have largely avoided an emphasis on biographical detail or a sustained account of production history. This decision is motivated in part by the existence of other useful resources for that kind of information. Anyone wishing to know more about the behind-the-scenes world of *The Thick of It* can find articles and interviews in print and online media without difficulty or listen to the excellent commentaries provided by the creative team as special features on the DVD releases of the programme. Choosing a different route, I have for the most part attempted to engage with the on-screen world of *The Thick of It* and treat it as a fictional reality. When I talk about a particular interior space, for example, I am more interested in it as a place inhabited by the programme's characters and less because it was actually a real-life BBC building or that interior action featured heavily in *The Thick of It* due to a tight production budget. Both of these facts happen to be repeated in various accounts of the programme and, while I find that kind of detail interesting, I am disinclined to relay such accounts again in these pages. Instead, I want to maintain the special critical intimacy of watching television that any viewer experiences: searching the screen to build knowledge of the programme rather than seeking out that knowledge elsewhere. As a result, I have not pursued any of *The Thick of It*'s production team for interview, which would be a legitimate option for a book devoted to a single television programme. I hope it will serve as a compliment to them that I am keener to engage with the on-screen characters they have created, rather than the individuals responsible for that creation.

I have, in the course of my writing, made two assumptions. Firstly, that most readers of this book will have seen (or intend to see) *The Thick of It* and will recognise the scenes I describe. As a consequence, I have refrained from providing lengthy plot synopses or drawn-out passages of contextualising detail. Secondly, that anyone who has enjoyed *The Thick of It* will know that it is funny and, indeed, will probably find its humour to be a key attraction. I have not, therefore, attempted to reassert the programme's comedy or pull it apart in any great detail. I trust that an appreciation of *The Thick of It*'s humour is something that we share already (although that appreciation can never be identical from viewer to viewer) and that further elaboration on my part would not enrich our pleasure.

1 Achievement

The Thick of It first aired in May 2005 on the BBC's 'alternative to mainstream broadcasting' channel, BBC Four (BBC Trust, 2014b). The final episode of its fourth series aired in September 2012 on the more mainstream BBC Two (BBC Trust, 2014a). The decision to shift the programme's broadcast channel from series three onwards, thus implicitly showcasing it to a larger audience, provides an indication of the BBC's confidence in *The Thick of It*: a recognition of its achievements in that seven-year period. The broadcaster's appreciation was mirrored elsewhere in the industry and beyond, with the programme gaining nominations and winning multiple awards, notably from the British Academy of Film and Television Arts and the Royal Television Society, as well as receiving sustained critical praise in the British media. Furthermore, by the end of the fourth series, the programme had made its successful transition to cinema in the 2009 film *In the Loop* and provided the inspiration (and the core creative team) for the acclaimed US show *Veep*. In this period, *The Thick of It* had so successfully depicted its subject matter – the unscrupulous backstage machinations of the British political system – that it had been embraced by members of that very system and by a large number of professionals wishing to pass comment on British politics. (Indeed, the extent to which 'The Thick of It' came to approach near-metonymic status as a phrase deployed in political commentary is a concern that we will return to in this chapter.)

Even this limited listing of the programme's accomplishments should begin to secure the notion that *The Thick of It* is frequently understood as an example of achievement in television by a range of different institutions and individuals. The admiration and recognition of these various sources has guaranteed a level of visibility for the programme, whereby its achievements are known and appreciated publicly by many diverse groups. A book dedicated solely to *The Thick of It* therefore, at the very least, courts the risk of becoming a somewhat extravagant exercise in reinforcing or even regurgitating that praise. We are entitled to ask whether such a volume might superfluously attempt to raise awareness of a programme that has already received and continues to receive very favourable attention: whether it makes a case that has been made a number of times before. Perhaps these are concerns that, in an era of vastly increased access to and awareness of television across a range of platforms, should occupy the thoughts of anyone seeking to engage meaningfully in television criticism. In previous years, studies have been made and books have been written about milestones of popular culture in part to address the fact that so little serious attention had been paid to them up to that point. In film, for example, Robin Wood's decision to write his landmark 1965 book on Alfred Hitchcock was motivated significantly by the critical neglect that director's work, and Hollywood cinema as a whole, had received at the time (Wood, 1965, pp. 7–43). And even as the case for works of cinema was being made successfully by figures like Wood, television continued to exist largely away from sustained critical attention, let alone appreciation. And so when John Fiske and John Hartley published their book, *Reading Television*, as late as 1978, they were still justifiably entitled to point out in their introduction that a debate about the value of television had barely begun, precisely as a result of a widespread lack of proper scrutiny (Fiske and Hartley, 1978, pp. 13–20).

The important interventions of writers like Wood, Fiske and Hartley take their place in an ever-increasing critical attentiveness towards film and television, bringing us to today's somewhat saturated coverage and critique found across social media, journalism, industry promotion and, indeed, academic publication. Given the range and diversity of commentary, the likelihood of a television programme going unnoticed or unappreciated (positively or negatively) has become increasingly remote.[1] In the case of *The Thick of It*, a spectrum of reflective and commemorative responses to the programme can be found with relative ease, spanning broadsheet newspaper retrospectives, industry magazine features, tabloid exclusives about celebrity viewers (Brad Pitt and Angelina Jolie, apparently), interviews with the cast and crew, blog discussions, dedicated Facebook pages, YouTube videos compiling favourite moments, even a series of Tumblr posts reimagining offensive lines from the programme as motivational poster designs.

Almost all of these sources seek to celebrate *The Thick of It* and all reveal a shared dedication to the programme's cultural significance and relevance. It follows, therefore, that any position one may wish to take in relation to the programme is almost certain to support and be supported by opinions held by individuals or groups somewhere. And,

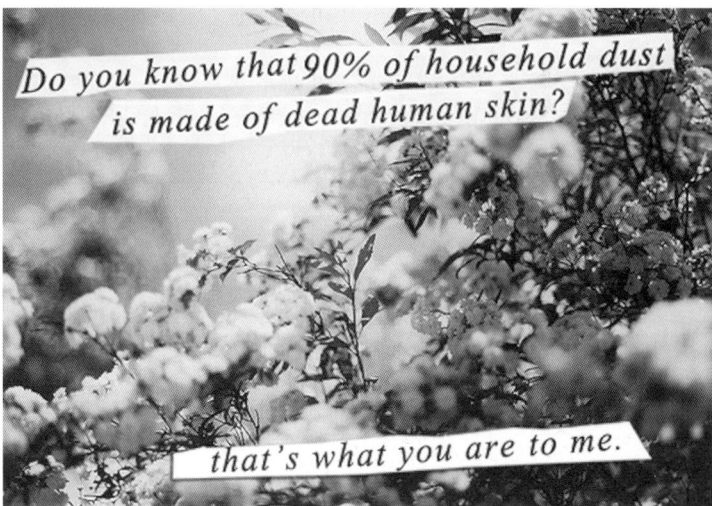

www.hipsterttoi.tumblr.com

in the case of *The Thick of It*, this is likely to be especially pertinent if we wish to promote the programme's value and achievement, given that its value and achievement are acknowledged regularly and widely.

If this is true, then it is also the case that widespread recognition and celebration of any television programme can at times provide a potential barrier to sustained critical analysis. Because a significant degree of agreement has ostensibly been reached on *The Thick of It*'s achievement, for example, there is perhaps a temptation to accept that consensus as a conclusion and withdraw from further comment. In revisiting *The Thick of It*, this book is revisiting something that is already known, valued and understood by its audience. In this sense, the arguments contained within these pages read *with* a broad critical consensus, rather than reading against it or seeking to rectify a perceived critical neglect. However, in order to avoid a bland or pedestrian celebration of the programme's achievements, it is necessary to think more carefully about the nature and form of those accomplishments: to structure and organise the ways in which we might wish to articulate them.

To that end, we can begin to view *The Thick of It*'s achievements in at least two broadly defined ways, each working in combination and each centred on the notion of resonance. Firstly, we can attend to the programme's *immediate resonance*: its ability to evoke powerfully the conditions of the historical, social and cultural moment in which it is produced. Secondly, we can think about its *wider resonance*: its ability to explore themes and issues that transcend those specific historical, social and cultural contexts. In approaching the first of those two definitions of resonance, we might very well contend that it is impossible for any television programme – or, indeed, any work of art – to fail to reflect these conditions in some way. However, *The Thick of It* enjoys an especially close and complex relationship to its moment of production. The programme's precise intertwining with the contexts of twenty-first-century British politics has been rightly lauded and, indeed, has become one of the main touchstones for the praise it has attracted. As a 2012 editorial in the *Observer* newspaper explains:

> When a chief whip on a bike is caught behaving out of order, when a prime minister is accidentally heard calling someone a bigot, or when a chancellor of the exchequer is caught fare-dodging on a train, there is only one thing to say: 'It is just like *The Thick of It*' we cry. (Editorial, 2012)

These editorial remarks encapsulate succinctly the complexities of *The Thick of It*'s relationship to contemporary political life. There is the suggestion that so accurate did the programme become in depicting its subject that reality and art became somehow merged in the minds of viewers, to the extent that events in politics were evaluated for their accuracy to the fictional events of *The Thick of It*, rather than only vice versa. This close interweaving of fact and fiction is one of the programme's celebrated hallmarks, and we can recognise it as being a central trait in the television work of its creator, Armando Iannucci.

In 1994, Iannucci collaborated with Chris Morris to devise and produce *The Day Today*, broadcast on BBC Two and adapted from their BBC Radio 4 series, *On the Hour*.[2] *The Day Today* is a surreal parody of news and current affairs programming that successfully mocks the often bombastic tone of that genre by covering a succession of comically absurd news items with the same straight-faced seriousness. And so headline stories such as 'Sacked chimney sweep pumps boss full of mayonnaise' or 'Prince Charles volunteers to put himself in prison to highlight the plight of Britain's jails' are delivered by Morris, playing the role of news anchor, with the recognisable staged sincerity and assumed gravitas of daily news bulletins. Other features in the programme would be equally nonsensical and outlandish, from Alan Partridge's (Steve Coogan) inept sports reports, to the bearded Rosie May's (Rebecca Front) ludicrous 'Enviromation' section, to Brant's (David Schneider) physical performances of the generic newspaper political cartoon. Although the content of *The Day Today* involves a degree of political commentary, inasmuch as its stories often ridicule political leaders of the era, the programme doesn't function primarily as political satire. Rather, it seeks principally to parody the codes and conventions of news programming itself, and part of that strategy involves inflating the style and delivery of that genre in order to make it preposterous. The programme's achievement therefore relies to a significant degree upon its awareness and deployment of a set of audiovisual design standards in news and current affairs, including tropes such as bombastic musical scoring and elaborate computer graphics, awkward jocular interplay between presenters, stories delivered by hosts roaming the studio floor and the aggressive interrogation of guests by a news anchor. Whilst in *The Day Today* these features were recognisable exaggerations of news broadcasts of 1994, the programme-makers could scarcely have anticipated that, in the years following its transmission, news programmes would come to replicate that overblown style and tone in their own content. Indeed, news reports became ever more stridently soundtracked as channels sought to carve out a recognisable identity for their broadcasts; dramatic developments in computer software led to the widespread integration of computer-generated graphics within all aspects of bulletins; attempts to make the news less austere 'un-anchored' presenters entirely from traditional news desks and encouraged a markedly more casual style of interaction between them; and even the BBC's interrogator-in-chief, Jeremy Paxman, began to self-consciously exploit the excesses of his maverick confrontational style in a manner at times mirroring that of Chris Morris's *The Day Today* anchor.

The consequence of these developments is that the comically overblown, absurd style and content of *The Day Today* begins to resemble a kind of blueprint for British news programming in the late twentieth and early twenty-first centuries. The programme not only parodied with great efficiency its chosen genre but also, perhaps inadvertently, demonstrated a near-prescient awareness of how that genre might develop in the future. And so, in 2007 when the BBC's local election coverage included a segment illustrating a potential Liberal Democrat gain in the vote entitled 'Ming's Bling' (named after the sexagenarian leader Sir Menzies Campbell), featuring a golden

the thick of it

BBC News Election Night 2007

computer-generated Campbell in an Ali G tracksuit gyrating awkwardly to a hip-hop soundtrack, parody and reality had become almost indistinguishable from each other. The segment looked and sounded like something from *The Day Today* in spite of the thirteen years that separate the broadcasts.

If developments in television news and current affairs meant that *The Day Today* retrospectively came to resemble a future version of the very object it sought to parody, it is perhaps to be expected that Armando Iannucci's television comedy work can sometimes be mistaken for 'straight' socio-political commentary. Occasionally, the nature of this confusion can be surprising. For example, on 12 February 2015, Iannucci appeared as a panellist on the BBC's flagship political debate programme, *Question Time*. On the panel was the United Kingdom Independence Party (UKIP) deputy chairman, Suzanne Evans. At one point in the recording, Evans responded to an audience question about the bland lack of distinction between the leaders of the main political parties. Part of her answer included the following: 'You know, I was watching a video on YouTube the other day and it segued a speech by Tony Blair with a speech with [*sic*] David Cameron. And you know what? They were saying exactly the same thing.' Given that Blair had ceased to be prime minister in 2007, the remark perhaps registers as slightly dated. More striking, however, is the fact that the sequence Evans was referring to could indeed be found on YouTube, but actually originated from Iannucci's own 2006 series *Time Trumpet*, co-created with Roger Drew and Will Smith. *Time Trumpet* offers a satire of the present day through the fictionalised device of a nostalgia show set in 2031 (thus simultaneously parodying a genre of television that had become somewhat ubiquitous in 2006). The segueing of Cameron and Blair's speeches does indeed carry the impact that Evans suggests, and is a skilful piece of editing. However, that a member of a political party should choose to reference it as a piece of political commentary nearly a decade after it was broadcast, oblivious to the fact that its co-creator was seated opposite her on the same panel, provides a strong indication of the honed accuracy and striking potency of Iannucci's comedy material. The studio audience and panel members of the 2015 *Question Time* broadcast were in tune with the notion that political leaders had come to resemble each other so closely that they were almost interchangeable, yet Iannucci had effectively pointed out this truth nine years earlier with such degrees of foresight and precision that Suzanne Evans should cite it as a reflection of the 2015 political landscape. The significant difference, of course, was that in Iannucci's (and his co-creators') hands, the comparison between Blair and Cameron is funny. In the sequence, the leaders' tired repetition of the word 'change' is carefully edited, leading them to recite the lyrics of David Bowie's 'Changes', and an actor (William Hoyland) playing a 2031 incarnation of New Labour's former director of communications, Alastair Campbell, bemoans Cameron's aping of Blair's prime ministerial style, from 'the way he used to hold his hands in front of his tits' to a more fundamental 'copying' of Blair's idea to be prime minister at all. Although neglecting to mention the original context of *Time Trumpet*, Evans's reference to the sequence demonstrates the clear potential for comedy to formulate sincere and powerful commentaries on political and social issues. In this instance, it is apparent that the commentary remains relevant years after its original broadcast, hence Evans's citation.

The prescience of *The Day Today* and *Time Trumpet* helps to establish Armando Iannucci as an especially perceptive observer of trends and movements in media, politics and society. This reputation is enriched by his role as creator of *The Thick of It*. Taking its inspiration from real political events, attitudes and rhetoric, the programme began to second-guess with uncanny accuracy the world of politics, leading to certain instances of life imitating art that the *Observer* editorial, cited above, alludes to. By the fourth series, the interplay between *The Thick of It*'s fictional world and the world of British politics had become consistent and complex. For example, the third episode of the series aired on 22 September 2012. One storyline involved the 'junior coalition partner' minister and his special adviser planning to set up a community micro-bank that would provide low-interest loans for small and fledgling businesses. Provisionally titled 'the We bank', the initiative would involve an initial capital investment of £2 billion of government funding. On 24 September 2012, Vince Cable, business secretary and member of the Liberal Democrat party (junior coalition partner in government), announced £1 billion of funding for a 'British business bank' to help small and medium-sized enterprises (Owen, 2012). Television production schedules dictate that this weird correspondence could only be a pleasing moment of serendipity for the programme-makers. Indeed, one of *The Thick of It*'s writers, Sean Gray, makes clear that the team have no covert access to government or opposition policy that might guarantee some advance knowledge. Instead, he explains, 'The truth is actually much more terrifying: we're making it up as we go along. Just like they are' (Gray, 2012). Gray's assertion offers the unsettling and enticing notion that both television writers and politicians are engaged in very similar processes of invention. Certainly, the fact that actual policy can be perceived as somehow replicating the events of fictional political comedy illustrates the close affinity that *The Thick of It* achieves with the reality it seeks to depict.

The propensity for *The Thick of It* to anticipate the actions and behaviours of politicians was not restricted to its fourth series, however. A scene in the 2007 special episode, 'The Rise of the Nutters', explored the scenario of a profoundly underprepared and inarticulate minister being interviewed by Jeremy Paxman on the BBC's *Newsnight* programme, a notoriously uncomfortable experience for real politicians. The result is junior minister Ben Swain (Justin Edwards) sweating, spluttering, stuttering and blinking his way through an excruciating encounter with Paxman. The scene successfully exploits the performances of real politicians, appearing on the programme, who had often verged on this level of ineptitude when placed under scrutiny. However, in June 2012, the inexperienced treasury minister Chloe Smith made an unfortunate appearance on *Newsnight* that resembled closely Swain's incompetence as she demonstrated a paralysing inability to manage the assorted pressures of the Paxman interview. In the aftermath of Smith's performance, commentators inevitably referenced *The Thick of It* in their analysis, pointing out once more the complex crossover between the worlds of political fiction and political fact (Neather, 2012). The fictional Ben Swain interview ordeal serves as a reflection upon how heavily prepared politicians usually are for television appearances and, indeed, we see Swain receiving an aggressive brand of media coaching from senior press officer Jamie McDonald (Paul Higgins) in role as Paxman that includes the improbable interjection 'Answer the question, you fat fuck!' Smith's disastrous *Newsnight* appearance suggests a lapse in any kind of thorough media training that, whilst a surprising occurrence, can be easily understood through a contextual frame provided by *The Thick of It*. Indeed, Smith's performance was read in the context of the Ben Swain scene immediately after it was broadcast: our perception of the reality influenced unavoidably by the fiction that had preceded it.

The conflation between *The Thick of It*'s fictional reality and real political life reached a somewhat unusual climax on 18 April 2012 when, in a session of Prime Minister's Questions in Parliament, the

the thick of it

Newsnight

leader of the opposition Ed Miliband included the following assessment of the government's recently announced Budget:

> Over the past month we have seen the charity tax shambles, the churches tax shambles, the caravan tax shambles, so we are all keen to hear the prime minister's view on why he thinks, four weeks on from the Budget, even people within Downing Street are calling it an omnishambles Budget.

On the face of it, Miliband's speech possesses a structured elegance that builds effectively through various mentions of 'shambles' to his central term 'omnishambles'. However, any public admiration for the delivery was soon tempered by the realisation that the word 'omnishambles' originated from an episode of *The Thick of It*. In the first episode of series three, the government's director of communications Malcolm Tucker (Peter Capaldi) includes the term in an abusive appraisal of claustrophobic minister Nicola Murray's (Rebecca Front) reluctance to enter a lift with him:

> That's great. That's fucking great. That's another fucking thing right there. Not only have you got a fucking bent husband and a daughter that gets taken to school in a fucking sedan chair, you're also fucking mental! Jesus Christ. See you, you're a fucking omnishambles, that's what you are. You're like that coffee machine, you know: from bean to cup, you fuck up.

Given the original context in which the term was delivered, Miliband's adopting of 'omnishambles' in political debate contains at least a degree of risk. There is not only the danger of association with Tucker's offensive delivery but also of association with a television programme that offers a scathing portrayal of the political establishment itself. And, in terms of its specific use within *The Thick of It*, there is a third risk, as the minister referred to as an 'omnishambles', Nicola Murray, would go on to win the opposition leadership by a very slim margin and then become plagued by poor public relations, social awkwardness (including an inability to walk convincingly) and low personal approval ratings. Given that Miliband won the leadership by a wafer-thin 50.65 per cent majority, endured poor public relations (including his inability to eat a bacon sandwich convincingly) and recorded very weak approval ratings (with a low of minus fifty-five in a November 2014 YouGov poll), there was potential for some awkward comparisons. Perhaps Miliband's advisers considered these hazards and, on balance, reasoned that the line was too strong – and too pertinent – to pass up. Certainly, given that cultural references in the House of Commons had tended previously to follow the tone of Prime Minister David Cameron's sexist use of insurance advertising slogan 'calm down, dear' as a rebuke to a female member of parliament (Wintour, 2011), there was little chance that the standard could be lowered. If so, the calculated risk paid off. The term was picked up in the mainstream media, was reused by other ministers in the Commons and 'omnishambles' was even named Word of the Year 2012 by the *Oxford English Dictionary*. Fiona McPherson, a member of the *OED* judging panel, revealed that 'omnishambles'

> was a word everyone liked, which seemed to sum up so many of the events over the last 366 days in a beautiful way. It's funny, it's quirky, and it has broken free of its fictional political beginnings, firstly by spilling over into real politics, and then into other contexts. (McPherson, 2012)

McPherson's elegant endorsement of 'omnishambles' provides a clear indication of *The Thick of It*'s influence, although the programme's writers might reinterpret her description of it 'spilling over into real politics' as a straightforward 'stolen by real politicians' (hence Iannucci's sardonic tweet on the day of Miliband's speech: 'Fantastic. With the royalties from Miliband's "omnishambles" quote we've now secured enough funding for a new series'). There was always a general acknowledgment that MPs watched and even enjoyed *The Thick of It*, but Miliband's speech made those suggestions concrete as his team seized upon and creatively borrowed a relatively obscure line from the programme, employing it skilfully for political point-scoring. By the final series of *The Thick of It*, a scenario had formed whereby the fictional television programme was providing material, acquired by whatever means, for the reality upon which it was based, thus inverting the relationship between art and actuality.

This close fusing of *The Thick of It*'s content to real political events gave rise to a situation whereby the title of the programme took on a kind of metonymical status. The *Observer* editorial, mentioned earlier, provides three real-life instances – a chief whip on a bike caught behaving out of order, a prime minister accidentally heard calling someone a bigot, or a chancellor of the exchequer caught fare-dodging on a train – that have no firm relevance to any event depicted in *The Thick of It*. Yet, each are understood in relation to the programme precisely because they capture a tone of political act that might be found within the fiction: 'It is just like *The Thick of It*.' Likewise, when the Public Administration Select Committee published its report on the role and behaviour of special advisers on 18 September 2012, its authors presumably chose the title 'Special Advisers in the Thick of It' in order to conjure notions of the kind of dubious practices found in the programme, and to plant the implicit suggestion that those questionable tactics might exist in real political life without adequate guidelines and protection (Public Administration Select Committee, 2012). *The Thick of It* therefore operates concurrently as a television programme title and a term that encompasses a particular type of political culture. Although falling short of the universally metonymic phrase 'Groundhog Day', for example, which derives from the 1993 Harold Ramis film of the same name but which has come to encapsulate a widely held sensation of repeating the same experience over and over again, *The Thick of It* has become a shorthand term in political commentary that describes, often without need for further elaboration, an event, attitude or behaviour that might be crass, clumsy or even corrupt.

We can therefore read *The Thick of It*'s close relationship to real political culture as evidence of the programme's immediate resonance. It is to be expected that this feature should attract the most attention in critical accounts of the programme and, certainly, experiencing the ways in which an episode corresponds with contemporary British politics (or, indeed, vice versa) is undoubtedly a major part of our viewing pleasure. There is a thrill in these kinds of relationships that define the programme as not only relevant but also influential: important. It seems reasonable, therefore, to suggest that this kind of immediacy might represent a significant aspect of *The Thick of It*'s achievement. However, as I have suggested, it is also possible to think about the programme's achievement in terms of its wider resonance: the extent to which the themes and issues explored extend above and beyond their original political and cultural contexts. If we are making a case for the programme's value, it is necessary to consider also what meaning it might retain when contextual details such as coalition governments, *Newsnight* interviews, Ed Miliband or David Cameron have seen their significance diminished or even become obsolete through the passage of time. What will *The Thick of It* mean when these things have lost some or perhaps all of their meaning for audiences? Will the programme lose its significance?

As a way of pursuing this question, we can turn our attention briefly to Orson Welles's 1941 film *Citizen Kane*. It is widely acknowledged that the film's central character, Charles Foster Kane (played by Welles), was at least loosely based upon the real-life figure of the American newspaper magnate William Randolph Hearst. And yet, the closeness of *Citizen Kane*'s story to the biographical details of this man's life rarely features as a central concern when the film is studied in detail. Indeed, when I have seen it taught in university classes (often as a key text on first-year film studies modules), the subject of Hearst as a potential influence for the narrative events is barely mentioned, if at all. One reason for Hearst's diminishing role in critical understandings of *Citizen Kane* may be that the film so readily offers such a diversity of ways in which it can be discussed: cinematography, soundtrack, screenplay, cast, spatial design, point of view, narrative form and, of course, authorship, before we even arrive at subjects such as patriarchy, allegory, modernism, national identity or psychoanalytical interpretation. *Citizen Kane*'s status as a masterpiece of cinema does not, then, necessarily rely upon an understanding of Hearst's role in its origins. Laura Mulvey, however, offers a potential means by which the Hearst narrative may retain its relevance, if not its specificity:

> While the Hearst model is important to the film on a now dated and superficial level as an act of iconoclasm, its strength lies not in personal detail but in its generality. The identifiable Hearst persona is used as a springboard for reflection on wider issues of American politics and myth, especially as personified by the yellow press. And then this broad

> perspective narrows down again to the personal, not this time to the
> interiority of William Randolph Hearst, but to a fictional American tycoon,
> complete with an unconscious which might, perhaps, be symptomatic
> of the repressed in American capitalism and its society. (Mulvey, 1992,
> pp. 30–1)

Mulvey's contention that the source material for a fictional work – in this case, the Hearst persona – can act as a 'springboard for reflection on wider issues', even when the significance of that source has become obscure over time, is especially pertinent when we return to *The Thick of It*. As we have seen, the programme aligns itself closely to its contemporaneous political climate and, as a result, involves a series of characters, events or institutions deriving from a factual reality. Spanning the final years of the Labour government and the early years of the Conservative/Liberal Democrat coalition, *The Thick of It* clearly makes strong reference to the internal fabric of those administrations, and to some of its key figures. It is possible, for example, to identify speculative real-life precedents for the programme's fictional characters in terms of either behaviour or role: Ken Clarke for Peter Mannion (Roger Allam), Steve Hilton for Stewart Pearson (Vincent Franklin), Lord Andrew Adonis for Lord Julius Nicholson (Alex Macqueen), Peter Mandelson for Steve Fleming (David Haig). The programme is also embedded in a culture of modern political spin. This culture was seen to intensify under the New Labour's rise to power as the role of press and communications became ever more crucial in an era when rolling 24-hour news superseded the daily cycle of print media. In *The Thick of It*, the character of Malcolm Tucker, the aforementioned director of communications, sits at the centre of this world, and many commentators have been quick to draw comparisons between Tucker and New Labour's own chief press secretary, Alastair Campbell. These comparisons perhaps find greatest relevance when the programme is adapted for Iannucci's 2009 film *In the Loop*, and Tucker becomes embroiled in illegally fabricating the case for war in a narrative that closely resembles Campbell's alleged role in the production of a 'dodgy dossier' that provided justification for the US/British-led invasion of Iraq in 2003 (O'Neill, 2002). *In the Loop* is discussed in detail in chapter five of this book. However, in the television programme itself, there are a series of resemblances between the pair that suggest Campbell to be at least a partial inspiration for Tucker. In some instances, Tucker's behaviour might be seen as a fictional exaggeration of Campbell's. For example, with the party in opposition in 1995, Campbell recollects tackling the public relations issue of Labour politicians sending their children to selective schools. Following Tony Blair's decision to send his son to the London Oratory School, Campbell was presented with the news that MP Harriet Harman was intending to follow a similar course:

> Peter Hyman [Labour speechwriter and political adviser] confirmed to me that Harriet was thinking of sending her second son to a grammar school. I exploded and wrote a letter advising her strongly against. I said it would result in political damage to herself; it would be awful for her son, because he would be thrust into the media spotlight; and it would damage the party at a time when the post-Oratory wounds were healing. (Campbell, 2010, p. 337)

It is not possible to ascertain whether Campbell's own recollection of his reaction involves a degree of sanitisation before it was published in his collected diaries. However, even this version reveals his vociferous response to potential public relations threats and the extent to which, in the presiding culture of spin, an MP's personal choices are almost immediately owned by the party's communications team. In the equivalent scene from *The Thick of It*, Tucker's response to Nicola Murray's suggestion that she might send her daughter to a local independent school is typically less compromising:

> Jesus H. Fucking Corbett. Do you honestly think ... do you honestly believe that, as a minister, you can get away with that? You are saying that all your local state schools, *all* the schools that this government has drastically improved, are knife-addled rape sheds. And that's not a big story? For fuck's sake! Sort it or abort it.

Campbell's writing of a strongly worded letter appears especially cordial, almost quaint, when placed alongside Tucker's vitriolic assault. *The Thick of It* effectively dramatises and creatively exaggerates the 'explosion' that Campbell alludes too, ripping apart any veneer of politeness by placing the minister in the room, face to face with a spin doctor who has no requirement or inclination to behave with either restraint or respect. And yet, at the heart of Campbell and Tucker's actions lies the same motivation, the same stark warning to the member of parliament: you are no longer in full control of your private life, and your choices are no longer personal to you. It is quite possible that Campbell's concern for Harman's political reputation and her son's wellbeing were entirely genuine. However, the final assertion that her decision would damage the party perhaps dilutes the duty of care he might otherwise have sought to exercise. Tucker's foul-mouthed tirade does at least dispense unequivocally with any perceived notions of honour and cuts straight to the heart of the issue: Murray is a minister first and foremost; her potential choice is a potential threat to her party and little else.

Aside from these synergies between Campbell and Tucker's modus operandi, there are further correspondences between the emotional and intellectual burden the job places upon each of them. Campbell's diary account of his time in the role is littered with instances in which he neglects his wife and children, suffers bouts of – at times serious – ill-health, loses sleep, experiences profound anxiety and generally allows the work to expand and consume nearly his whole existence. These reflections naturally occupy relatively little space in relation to his discussion of the main business of political life but, nevertheless, slight details provide telling insights. For example, Campbell begins New Year's Day 1995 in the following way:

> Woke up early anxious about the DB situation [David Blunkett, shadow education secretary, had previously inadvertently suggested that a future Labour government might tax school fees]. Fiona [Millar, Campbell's partner] was determined I get some rest, so unplugged all the phones

> upstairs. I just lay there listening to them ring in the rest of the house so got up to begin another crap day. (Campbell, 2010, p. 121)

And, in the immediate afterglow of Labour's election success in 2001, he offers the following appraisal in a single diary entry for Friday, 15 June: 'I felt like I had some kind of post-natal depression. We'd won the election but every day since it had felt like swimming through shit' (Campbell, 2011, pp. 643–4). These sentences reveal not only the extent to which Campbell's personal life was invaded by the demands of his job (especially as his tenure coincided with the growth of a 24-hour news and mobile communications culture) but also the melancholy that could taint periods in which this relentless pace subsided, stealing the joy even from moments of victory.

Characteristically, these sentiments become bleaker and more venomous in *The Thick of It* as Malcolm Tucker indulges in an equivalent moment of reflection when responding to a passing remark from his colleague, Ollie Reeder (Chris Addison):

> You know fuck all about me! I am totally beyond the realms of your fucking tousled-haired fucking dim-witted compre-fucking-hension. I don't just take this fucking job home you know. I take this job home, it fucking ties me to the bed, and it fucking fucks me from arsehole to breakfast. Then it wakes me up in the morning with a cupful of piss, slung in my face, slaps me about the chops to make sure I'm awake enough so that it can kick me in the fucking bollocks. This job has taken me in every hole in my fucking body. Malcolm is gone. You can't know Malcolm because Malcolm is not here! Malcolm fucking left the building fucking years ago! This is a fucking husk. I am a fucking host for this fucking job.

Campbell's sense that his role is akin to 'swimming through shit' is thus exaggerated wildly in the form of Tucker's powerful and unsettling extended metaphor. Crossovers of this kind in the personal reflections of the real person and the fictional character provide perhaps serendipitous opportunities for comparison, inviting the suggestion that Tucker might be an effective elaboration of Campbell's own behaviours and attitudes. And yet, forcing any direct correlation between the two figures might risk providing a limited representation of the programme's achievements (and, perhaps, an equally limited view of Alastair Campbell). We should consider what is at stake in the assumption that Tucker is somehow a straightforward portrayal of a single, real-life entity. Adopting this view would, for example, require us to ignore *The Thick of It*'s assiduous resistance to any mention of actual political parties or figures. This deliberate strategy is made yet more apparent when other real names and institutions, particularly from news and popular culture, are referenced constantly: *EastEnders*, BBC Radio 5, the *Guardian* newspaper, James May, Jeremy Paxman, *The Big Breakfast*, *Star Wars*, Sky News, Jim Bowen, *Newsnight*, *GQ* magazine and so on. Yet, the programme is very careful to shun any mention of Labour, Conservative or the Liberal Democrats, of Blair, Brown or Thatcher. In doing so, *The Thick of It* avoids becoming a one-dimensional satirising of any particular regime and, as a consequence, avoids a potential narrowing of its dramatic aims. Malcolm Tucker is not simply a functioning impression of Alastair Campbell, and when, for example, he delivers that abject assessment of himself as a 'fucking host for this fucking job' in the final episode of series four, he has surely developed into a fully rounded, profoundly idiosyncratic character in his own right. This is due to a combination of the programme's exceptional writing talent, Peter Capaldi's meticulous performance of the role and a character arc that spans series and takes Tucker from the height of his powers in government to disgrace and dejection as his party sits in opposition and he faces criminal proceedings. Indeed, as episodes accumulate, Campbell as a potential source of inspiration seems to recede further and further into the background as Tucker's particular narrative takes centre stage.

Aside from the need to preserve the fictional integrity of its characters and plot, *The Thick of It*'s avoidance of direct political citation also seems to emphasise the breadth of its situations and themes, to the extent that they might conceivably be applied to a range of different political figures, and even different administrations. This is important given that, certainly in the first three series of *The Thick of It*, the programme might risk being read only as a straight response to certain attitudes and behaviours employed by New Labour in the years leading up to its broadcast in 2005. It is certainly the case that the birth of New Labour as a 'brand' coincided with the intensified awareness through increased visibility of the spin doctor. In 1998, a year after Labour came into office, author and party activist Paul Richards chose to publish a book entitled *Be Your Own Spin Doctor*. The title selection for this mainstream publication presumes a corresponding mainstream understanding of what a spin doctor might be, and this awareness had been built up through New Labour's ascent to power in 1997. Much of this awareness was created in media coverage and, given the close mutual reliance between political communicators and media institutions, we might speculate that journalists were drawn to the workings of spin doctors at least partially for solipsistic reasons: effectively talking about their own professional world and, in the process, reinforcing the importance of the media to the success of the political machine.

We might concede that the increased media interest in political spin was due to a genuine increase in the activities of the Labour Party in the 1990s. However, it isn't necessarily the case that one individual can be credited with those efforts. Campbell certainly became a lightning rod for accusations of political spin, perhaps because of his previous employment as a journalist, his decision to remain in his role as Labour moved from the relative shadows of opposition to the intense spotlight of government, his apparent desire to maintain a public profile of his own, or ultimately because of his alleged involvement in 'sexing up' the case for war in Iraq. But it would be fatuous to suggest that Campbell was the sole architect of New Labour's communications strategy, especially in its early years. Peter Mandelson, for example, played an active role in shaping the New Labour brand and managing public perceptions of it through the media. However, as Mandelson's status as a member of parliament led him in various different directions (taking in Secretary of State for Trade and Industry, Secretary of State for Northern Ireland and membership of the House of Lords), perhaps his role as media strategist faded from memory or interest. This situation became exacerbated when Mandelson was embroiled in controversies that forced him to resign from government on two separate occasions, thus reinventing him as a very different focus for media interest.

If a culture of political spin cannot be attributed solely to the efforts of Alastair Campbell, it is also the case that 'spin' was not invented by New Labour, and was not restricted to the period in which Campbell was in post. Nicholas Jones, for example, has looked beyond that era to illustrate the ways in which Bernard Ingham, Margaret Thatcher's chief press secretary, helped to shape public perceptions of the miners' strike in 1985 through a series of carefully coordinated press briefings (Jones, 1999, pp. 11–12). Furthermore, historian Martin Moore traces the origins of modern spin back to the post-World War II Labour government, but goes even further by making the point that:

> spin, in the political sense, is simply the way in which a government, any government, seeks to present its actions in the most favourable light. Every government spins. It is the means by which they maintain and enhance their power. Henry VIII led a large-scale propaganda programme to convince his subjects that Catholicism was no longer the true religion. The Victorians very successfully diverted industrial unrest at home by extolling the successes of imperialism abroad. (Moore, 2006, p. 1)

Viewing political spin in these broader historical contexts makes clear that *The Thick of It* does not begin and end with Alastair Campbell, or even New Labour. Indeed, further resemblances between the programme and reality occur well after Campbell's departure (and even after Labour had left office). There are, for example, more than faint traces of Malcolm Tucker in the behaviour of Damian McBride, special adviser to Gordon Brown until 2009, as he blithely briefed against party colleagues or leaked confidential details to the press for political gain (McBride, 2013). Similarly, Tucker's arrest in the programme's final episode resembles closely the demise of Andy Coulson, David Cameron's director of communications, whose political career concluded with his arrest and subsequent sentencing in 2014 for conspiracy to intercept voicemails (O'Carroll, 2014).

    Considering *The Thick of It* beyond a narrow period in British politics may point us towards the programme's potential longevity: its ability to remain relevant even when certain specific contexts have changed or lost their significance. Indeed, if we return to Laura Mulvey's contention that the strength of *Citizen Kane* relies upon its generality, rather than its specificity, we might well argue that moving away from an assessment of *The Thick of It* as only a product of its time can broaden and, importantly, enrich our understanding of the programme. *The Thick of It* encapsulates a series of behaviours and attitudes found across decades, perhaps even centuries, of political communication, and we might view this as part of its wider resonance. There is a further layer to this resonance, however, as the programme provides an illustration of behaviours and attitudes found outside that professional sphere. Although certainly idiosyncratic in its style and form, the kind of verbal bullying Malcolm Tucker deals in is not necessarily the preserve of government spin doctors. We might observe it in a range of professions and it is unsurprising that Capaldi found inspiration for the character elsewhere: Hollywood agents and producers, notably Harvey Weinstein of Miramax (Wardrop, 2012). Likewise, we can recognise that Nicola Murray's incompetence is not confined especially to her positions as cabinet minister or leader of the opposition. Our appreciation of these characters can certainly involve an awareness of British politics in the years of *The Thick of It*'s production, but it is not dependent upon that awareness. In this way, although recognising political references within the programme can be fun, that recognition may not be essential to its enduring quality and achievement. This makes sense if we consider *The Thick of It* alongside other television situation comedies, where an in-depth knowledge of dreary stationery suppliers in Slough or deranged hotel owners in Torquay, for example, is not central to our comprehension and enjoyment.

Thinking about *The Thick of It* in terms of its wider resonance can help to frame a discussion around thematic and aesthetic structures at work within the programme. A conversation based predominantly upon the programme's direct links to a specific political era and climate might risk overlooking these features by jumping to the immediate significance of the events on screen (the programme's immediate resonance) without necessarily considering the ways in which those events are represented to us. In short, this narrower view neglects to evaluate *The Thick of It* as television art and instead frames it as only political commentary. The following pages of this book will work on an assumption that the artistic design of the programme contributes significantly to its wider resonance. I suggest implicitly that, as with the universality of its characters and situations, the aesthetic and thematic design of *The Thick of It* may secure its enduring relevance and power even when its immediate contextual setting becomes a distant memory.

2 Style

Episode one. Scene one. Exterior shot. A man makes his way from a parked car, ascends a small flight of steps and enters a building through a set of revolving doors. The journey occupies just nine seconds of screen time and consists of four rapidly edited shots (see page 47). This staccato visual pattern creates fragments of detail, each cut adding a new layer of information. Signs and meanings begin to accumulate. The car is chauffeured: the departing passenger is of some importance. He is handed two red briefcases: a minister of the British government. A large printed sign is clear above the revolving doors: he is Secretary of State for a Department of Social Affairs. The relaying of information in this very brief opening segment is especially efficient, allowing the viewer to become quickly orientated within a specific fictional setting. And yet, this efficiency extends to the establishment of a particular tone in the scene and a defined perspective on the events depicted. Any suggestion of a grandiose ministerial entrance is not merely resisted but obliterated. We barely see this man's face as he makes his way towards the entrance. This is partly a matter of spatial positioning, the camera remaining behind him as he moves away from us. It is partly due to the actor's performance that restricts movements and utterances to blank understatement (just a few curt, monotone utterances of 'morning' or 'thank you' as he makes his way from the car). And it is partly due to a costume choice of 'regulation' dull suit and tie that paints the man as sartorially indistinct. But the character's anonymity is also, perhaps mainly, attributable to that especially brisk editing rhythm that fractures any sustained appreciation of the individual, pulling away or reframing the image when the camera might have lingered or moved in. This pace of cutting not only impacts upon the identity of the character, the manner in which he is shown to us, but also *creates* his identity, to the extent that a montage of splintered and barely held images *become* the man.

Even when, seconds later, we are presented with an actual static image of this character by way of an official framed photograph hanging in the lobby of the building's interior, we are afforded only a fleeting glimpse as the camera hurries us past. We then cut to a side view of the same man in the flesh, moving through the interior space in a slightly hastened fashion, looking weary and already harassed as he continues his morning journey (see page 48). The potential gravitas and, perhaps, pomposity of the conventionally posed photograph portrait is undercut by its diminished placement within a sequence of shots, the brevity of its treatment and its sharp contrast with the far less cosmetically constructed reality of the portrait's subject as he walks past it. This comparison encapsulates the central strategy of this short sequence and, indeed, of *The Thick of It* in general: to strip away the veneer of political figures' stage management and concentrate entirely upon their unplanned, unmanaged selves. It is not unusual for television programmes depicting politicians to seek out an uncompromising or critical perspective on their actions, of course. We might say, for example, that both the UK and US versions of *House of Cards* (1990/2013–) make this their brutal and unremitting goal. Each goes to elaborate lengths to outline the moral corruption of its central character, Francis Urquhart (Ian Richardson) in the UK original and Frank Underwood (Kevin Spacey) in the US adaptation, as they rise to the position of prime minister and president, respectively, through their duplicitous and degraded manoeuvres. And yet, damning as these portraits of political leaders are, the characters are nevertheless afforded significant degrees of authority, influence and even gravitas. Each incarnation of *House of Cards* works on the basic premise that the actions of politicians matter, whether the intentions are noble or malevolent. This attitude is revealed in a consistent representational style that elevates and privileges the central protagonists. We can see this at work in the very first moments of the UK *House of Cards*, which, like *The Thick of It*, features a framed image of a politician but opts for an entirely different manner of depiction and, as a consequence, achieves a very different aim.

The scene begins before the title sequence. We fade up from darkness to a high-angle shot of Urquhart sitting alone at a desk in his office. The single light source, a brass desk lamp, picks out symbols of grandeur and opulence: oak-panelled walls, heavy velvet curtains, an antique carriage clock that ticks peacefully in the background, an ornate writing set and inkwell on a walnut desk and a crafted chess table positioned to the left of the seated Urquhart. He sits in pensive thought, elbows resting on the surface of the desk and hands clasped together just below his chin in a pose resembling the conventional gesture of prayer. He reaches to pick up a silver picture frame from the desk and we cut to an over-the-shoulder close-up of the object, revealing it to be a black-and-white photograph of a smiling Margaret Thatcher wearing a collared, chequered jacket and holding a large bouquet of flowers. The frame carries the embellishment of an engraved crown that, due to its positioning over the photograph, appears just above Thatcher's head, as though elevating her briefly to the position of royalty. There is silence as this image is held and then Ian Richardson's slow, sonorous baritone delivers the programme's first, and crucial, line: 'Nothing lasts for ever.' He falls into silence again, the ticking of the clock becoming more pronounced in the background, and then places the frame face down on the desk with measured deliberation. And then the camera readjusts slightly to frame Urquhart's face more fully as, somewhat unexpectedly, he turns to face the camera: turns to face *us*. From this position, he allows a slight smile to form and linger, tinged with a faint sparkle of malice, as he discloses to us: 'Even the longest, most glittering reign must come to an end someday.' The line is held and we cut to the titles.

bfi tv classics

House of Cards (1990)

The connotations of this brief opening sequence are relatively clear: Thatcher, the reigning prime minister, has been deposed and Urquhart consigns her to history as he does away with her image by facing her photograph down on the desk.[3] The scene establishes a relationship between this woman and Urquhart: he is the force dispatching her to the past and a causal link is created between the two that proposes him as the figure to take her place. His address to camera performs the function of a theatrical soliloquy as it represents a moment of disclosure between character and audience. Rather like a succinct version of the opening speech in Shakespeare's *Richard III*, Urquhart's short address refers minimally to the formation of a plan. And following the nature of Shakespeare's central character, his dangerous half-smile reveals a trace of villainous intent, even if his actual words are brief and, at this stage, somewhat ambiguous. Indeed, throughout the series, Urquhart's moments of direct address to camera always hold something back, keeping the character one step ahead of the viewer and maintaining his status as calculating and duplicitous even when he is apparently confiding in us. In this way, his actions chime with Tom Brown's assertion that 'were direct address used only when a character is telling the truth, its impact on the concerns of many dramas would be rather deadening ... Direct address may sometimes, rather, be a gesture of ingenuousness' (Brown, 2013, pp. 14–15).

There can be little doubt that this scene in *House of Cards* aims to present a less than flattering depiction of politicians. The embossed crown that appears above the head of Thatcher, for example, is surely an ironic comment on that prime minister's gradual fall from grace: the irretrievable slipping of the coronet. Indeed, by the time the programme aired in November 1990, that decline had led to a Conservative leadership election being called, a move that would eventually result in Thatcher's resignation that same month. Likewise, we are unlikely to miss the fact that Urquhart's address to camera provides a tangible flicker of the ruthlessness that will define his character as the episodes progress. And yet, despite the respective critical portrayals of the politicians on screen, the programme also builds a sense of gravitas around these two individuals. At the time of broadcast, viewers could hardly be unaware of Thatcher's own powerful influence over British politics, and the simple inclusion of her image immediately conjures notions of her unyielding authority: the soft petals of her bouquet striking a contrast against the 'iron lady'. Relegating Thatcher to a still, black-and-white image and having Urquhart display a control over that image by facing it down on the desk serves to elevate his own status with particular efficiency. The decisiveness of the move hints at a change of regime and, as a consequence, a shifting of power from one leader to the next (although Urquhart's path to the leadership becomes slightly more circuitous as he first has to depose Thatcher's immediate successor). Taken in the light of the series as a whole, this small gesture carries profound weight, setting out Urquhart's ambitions and illustrating that even minimal actions and thoughts have important consequences.

Despite its overtly cynical stance, therefore, the scene also carries the underlying assertion that the work of politicians matters. The settled style of depiction allows Urquhart the time and space to perform, with no sharp cuts or unsteady camerawork disrupting or directing his flow. Indeed, we are given the distinct sense that we have been allowed into his inner sanctum, replete with its trappings of refinement, and that the nature of our access is dictated by a pace that he sets. Hence, the edits and camera movements are timed with Urquhart's actions. As the sequence concludes, his status in this composition is elevated further when he addresses the audience directly, his features almost filling the frame in close-up, as though he had momentarily taken ownership of the entire *mise en scène*.

The poise of Urquhart's introduction contrasts sharply, therefore, with the relative lack of distinction afforded to the minister in the opening scene of *The Thick of It*. Here, the camerawork and editing instead seem to work against any sense of power or control he might seek to exert in his role. Even when he is named as Cliff Lawton (Tim Bentinck) and greeted by a member of his staff, civil servant Terri Coverley (Joanna Scanlan), his presence is no more pronounced. He continues to be framed with his back to the camera or in medium-long shot, the staccato editing pattern that cuts through his words and actions is maintained and the camera manoeuvres freely around the space, never settling on Cliff for more than a few seconds. His reduced prominence within this representational style is complemented by a pronounced lack of professional consideration shown to him by Terri. She initially takes his red boxes from him in the lobby but then hands them back when they reach his office, because she does not personally want to encounter his first visitor of the morning, Malcolm Tucker. Terri's assertive manner as she holds the boxes out to Cliff and the awkwardness of his response effectively shift the balance of power from member of parliament to civil servant. A yet more dominant element is introduced immediately, however, when the minister becomes unusually nervous and agitated on discovering that none of his staff has provided refreshments for Tucker. Given Terri's earlier reluctance to even be in the same room as the man, Tucker is clearly established as the most important figure in this set-up. As Cliff's loud protestations are met with casual indifference by Terri and another colleague, he is placed firmly at the foot of this hierarchy, and he only weakens his demand for rectification by attempting to second-guess his visitor's preferences and settling on the laughable provision of 'a pile of fruit and lots of coffee' for Tucker. Again, the camera repeatedly pulls away from Cliff during this exchange and the framing often places him in the background of the shot, accentuating his inability to assert his authority. At this point, style and story are working to undermine the minister in a relatively understated way, although we might find cause to overlook the manner of Cliff's representation and perhaps pass it off as symptomatic of the programme's intention to inject pace and urgency into these early moments. However, it is when Cliff enters his office and encounters Tucker that this pattern of emasculation becomes targeted and intensified.

Tucker's latent superiority over Cliff is emphasised even before the two characters engage with each other. Firstly, the simple fact that Tucker is already waiting in the minister's office places him in a position of assumed authority as he implicitly claims ownership of the space. Secondly, as we see Cliff enter his office, Tucker is heard inside on the phone saying: 'No, he's useless. He's absolutely useless. He is; he's useless. He's as useless as a marzipan dildo.' The audiovisual match here creates an ambiguous relationship between Cliff's entrance and Tucker's repeated use of the word 'useless', implying that one man may indiscreetly be describing the other. However, this underlying tension dissipates somewhat as Tucker offers a friendly acknowledgment to Cliff and ends his phone conversation with the deferential explanation: 'Gotta go, Minister's just walked in!' The two men shake hands and quickly settle into an exchange of small talk. The scene is still depicted in a style similar to the episode's opening as the camera sweeps around the space and the edits continue to break up the flow of speech and action but, rather than only Cliff being caught in this frenetic arrangement, we get the sense that both men are implicated. Once more, we might suggest that the programme's style functions primarily to successfully bind its characters together within a frantically paced fictional world. The show of cordial equality between Tucker and Cliff is maintained even when the conversation moves to the latter's extremely negative press coverage and a reference is made to a *Daily Mail* headline: 'LAWTON DANGLES BY A THREAD'. Tucker is reassuring: 'You're doing a bloody good job here, Cliff ... The PM likes you personally. I like you personally. And we have absolutely no desire to get rid of you.' We might begin to form the impression of two men standing against a barrage of negative press attention (the *Daily Mail* headline is one of many similar attacks) that is perhaps a hallmark of contemporary political life. In this context, the scene's reeling, penetrating style might come to symbolise that external pressure, stabbing away at the characters and breaking their actions apart. After the discussion of the papers and Tucker's reassurances, the two shake hands as though sealing their unified stance against the pernicious glare of the world outside.

    And then everything changes. Tucker continues to talk. He builds to an explanation that the endless headlines are starting to make the government look weak and that is why Cliff has to go. From this almost casual mention of resignation, the words and plans begin to snowball. Tucker has told the lobby he's going, a farewell at Number 10 will commence in twenty minutes, the title 'minister' no longer applies to Cliff, and Tucker has already written his letter of resignation, which he flops down unceremoniously onto Cliff's desk. Suddenly, Tucker has become the barrage. Capaldi allows a vocal force to creep into his sentences, sharpening consonants and puncturing vowels. The pace of his speech picks up, running in time with the rapid slices of the edit and the swooping, shifting camera. Here, performance style and visual style become fused, bringing together this central character and the programme's central representational strategy. We appreciate now that the opening minutes of the episode have been leading to this climax: that the gradual undermining of Cliff's character has built towards the cool humiliation being dealt to him by Tucker.

The synchronicity between Tucker and the programme's chosen style becomes yet more apparent when, bewildered by the onslaught, Cliff attempts to bargain with his colleague-turned-adversary. He suggests that 'Tom from [the Department of] Transport' take his place in the firing line but Tucker explains uncompromisingly that this is not an option and that Transport is more important than the Department of Social Affairs. In order to illustrate his point, he begins to distractedly list all the things that transport involves: cars, buses, trucks – at which point Cliff, unwisely, loses his temper and interjects: 'I know what transport fucking entails!' These words are left to hang in the air as we cut to a reverse shot of Tucker's face in close-up (see page 48). He stares impassively at Cliff, eyes narrowing slightly as seconds of silence accumulate. The sudden halt in the flow of the scene conveys the sense that Cliff's outburst has breached some unspoken (and unequal) protocol that hitherto existed between the men. Tucker's blank gaze, framed in close-up, registers this fact but then a sudden crash-zoom brings us in yet closer to him as a subtle change begins to form across his features (see page 48). He tilts his head slowly in a slight downwards motion, his mouth tightens into a teeth-clenched grimace and his unblinking stare becomes tinged with visible malice as it remains targeted upon the minister. This newly framed image of Tucker begins to reveal those aspects of the character's dangerous brutality that will come to define him in this episode and those that follow. (Indeed, from this moment on, any veneer of conviviality is dispensed with as Tucker's mode of address shifts to naked aggression and threat. The effects are both caustic and comic. Tucker snarls, for example, that: 'I have written some very nice things about you in the PM's reply to your resignation. Some very nice fucking things indeed! I had a lump in my throat!' whilst jabbing a finger menacingly at his own neck, thus layering a potentially sentimental statement with physical and verbal antagonism.) The sustained close-up of Tucker illustrates the extent to which the scene's style of depiction has become attuned to his actions and attitudes. The frenetic pace of the sequence is suspended for a moment in order to capture the character's own moment of stillness, to register in detail the effect Cliff's outburst has upon him and to externalise a series of dark emotions he experiences in response. The close alignment of character and style makes Tucker the epicentre of the scene's aesthetic composition. He is in time with its rhythms and movements, to the extent that his pause signals a temporary break in the flow of action. And when he launches back into his eviscerating method of delivery, barking orders at Cliff, gesticulating wildly, punctuating sentences with spittle-flecked expletives, the camerawork and editing pick up the pace again, conspiring with Tucker as they frame his unrelenting attack on the hapless minister.

With this in mind, we might say that the programme attaches us to Tucker at the same time as it distances us from Cliff. The fusion between character and style creates a further bond between character and audience, tying us into his actions and reactions – often at the expense of those other individuals in scenes. This process evokes some aspects of Murray Smith's work on the ways in which we engage with characters in cinema and, particularly, his notion of 'alignment' as a central facet of engagement. For Smith, the term alignment 'describes the process by which spectators are placed in relation to characters in terms of access to their actions, and to what they know and feel' (Smith, 1995, p. 83). And in television, as with film, it is representational style that offers the principal means for an audience to gain access to the actions, knowledge and feelings of characters. V. F. Perkins's formative concept of synthesis, 'where there is no distinction between how and what, content and form', holds value here, as surely our understanding of anything we experience on screen is always reliant upon the way in which that thing is shown to us: the techniques employed in its representation (Perkins, 1993, p. 133). In terms of stylistic choices facilitating character engagement, Smith rightly points out that a common critical misstep is to make the assumption that only the most direct visual manifestations of character point of view, namely point-of-view shots, can foster alignment (Smith, 1995, p. 156). In the case of *The Thick of It*'s opening scenes, we can see that subtle shifts in a remarkably complex and erratic visual style can effectively privilege one character's perspective over another's without needing to align literally with his physical viewpoint. From this moment on, we are inescapably with Tucker as the programme's style places us in close alignment with his character.

The suggestion that the style of *The Thick of It*'s opening moments can be related to an underlying representational strategy is useful in at least two ways. Firstly, it helps to determine the ways in which the programme handles its hierarchy of characters; how it prioritises individuals with a degree of subtle complexity through framing and editing choices. Secondly, identifying that there is a selective purpose to *The Thick of It*'s visual style is important because, by the time the programme aired in 2005, the use of sharp edits and unsteady camera movements was hardly novel in British television comedy. For example, although possessing a notably more settled aesthetic composition than a programme like *The Thick of It*, *The Royle Family* (1998–2012) nevertheless played a significant role in migrating situation comedy away from the standard studio-based arrangement and towards a more 'naturalistic' aesthetic style. This was achieved partly through a script that captured precisely the rhythms and breaks of everyday speech, partly through a dedication to realism that eschewed conventional sitcom features such as a stage set and laughter track and partly through a dexterous camera set-up that framed the space of the Royles' front room from a variety of angles and distances as the programme sought to interrogate the actions and reactions of its characters in lingering detail. In this way, at least in terms of style, it can be said that *The Royle Family* adopted certain trends found in television drama. An episode from programmes such as *This Life* (1996–7 and 2007) in the UK or *ER* (1994–2009) in the US, for example, might possess many of these qualities in an equivalent attempt to evoke a more realistic fictional experience. This can be read as not only an attempt to capture the often exhaustive pace of characters' professional and social lifestyles in both programmes (lawyers and doctors, respectively) but also as a means of representing their complex psychological perspectives as every gesture and glance becomes magnified and intensified in a pattern of intrusive fractured edits. It follows that, when situation comedies like *The Royle Family* began to embrace and re-employ the quasi-realist aesthetic of television drama, there was a corresponding shift towards a more psychologically authentic portrayal of characters. In episodes, significant emphasis is placed upon the subtle meanings behind nuances of phrase and expression at the expense of the more traditional structuring of dialogue towards the overt delivery of key punchlines. This became an influential approach in television comedy, with programmes like *Him & Her* (2010–13) and *Roger and Val Have Just Got In* (2010–12) constituting more recent extensions of a pared-down, undramatic style.

A second, related development in situation comedy involved the incorporation of certain aesthetic tropes from the reality television genre, particularly the newly emerged docusoap subgenre. In the UK, programmes such as *That Peter Kay Thing* (1999) and then *The Office* (2001–3) pioneered this trend, utilising conventions found in the seminal docusoaps *Airport* (1996–2008), *Driving School* (1997), *The Cruise* (1998) and the plethora of commissioned titles that followed (Kilborn, 2003, p. 89). Consequently, we can recognise features shared between these sitcoms and docusoaps, such as a focus on workplaces (and often the banality of everyday routine), a consistent mode of self-conscious direct address engendered by the on-screen participants' awareness of their 'role' within a programme's narrative, certain 'codes of "authenticity" (natural lighting, hand-held camera work, sometimes surprised by the action etc.)' and 'cheaper, easier subject matter' (Walters, 2005, p. 63). Indeed, in docusoaps, those stylistic 'codes of authenticity' went hand in hand with cheapness as real-life situational drama (and comedy) was – for obvious reasons – captured inexpensively without rehearsal or set-up, making features such as natural lighting and handheld cameras a practical necessity. This consequently gave rise to an unstable compositional mode as production crews strived to keep pace with the unfolding action, sometimes literally racing to keep their subjects in frame or else, more frequently, utilising sharp pans and swift zooms to catch moments of spontaneous drama. As conventions of this kind were incorporated into television comedy, it followed that an apparently unstructured and unplanned aesthetic style became synonymous with notions of realism and authenticity.

It would be easy, therefore, to see *The Thick of It* as simply another offering in a saturated field of 'naturalistic' television comedies. Such a conviction might be deepened further when we consider that Iannucci had already adopted this formal style some years earlier in his role as writer, director and producer for *I'm Alan Partridge* (1997– 2002), which depicted its titular character (played by Steve Coogan) in the manner of a fly-on-the-wall documentary (whilst retaining more conventional tropes such as a title sequence and audience laughter). Yet, such an assessment would fail to account for *The Thick of It*'s inventive deployment of these formal characteristics. In *The Thick of It*, the spontaneous immediacy that naturalistic television comedy can provide is utilised to create an entire fictional world infused with an especially relentless and brutal pace. The interrogative lens, for example, does not create a sympathetic intimacy, as with *The Royle Family* (Zborowski, 2013, pp. 127–8), or highlight characters' self-conscious awareness of their relationship to the camera, as with *The Office* (Walters, 2005, pp. 68–96). Rather, it becomes a key component within the programme's distinctive breathless intensity, combining with the often frantic tempo of the editing to create an unyielding rhythm that complements the actions of some characters and consumes the actions of others. The opening scene between Tucker and Cliff emphasises this strategy as the representational style empowers the former but emasculates the latter. (It follows that Cliff is quickly evacuated from the narrative and, in a telling illustration of a minister's potential dispensability within this world, his successor, Hugh Abbot (Chris Langham), is depicted entering the Department of Social Affairs in a series of almost identical shots.) Tucker remains at the epicentre of the programme's aesthetic approach and the bond between character and style endures. Other characters share this affinity with the programme's frenetic style, some more consistently than others. Whilst it could be said that Cliff's replacement, Hugh, remains on the whole contrastingly unenergetic and distanced, in large part due to Langham's precisely judged depiction of his character as consistently weary and deflated, special advisers Ollie Reeder and, to a lesser extent, Glenn Cullen (James Smith) are more willingly drawn into Tucker's ferocious kineticism. In the second episode of series two, however, all three become embroiled in one of his manoeuvres, providing a useful example of how various characters can become complicit with the programme's vigorous style at the same time as they fall in with Tucker's actions.

The four men (Tucker, Hugh, Glenn and Ollie) are assembled in Hugh's office and, within a couple of minutes, Tucker conceives of and executes a plan to cut dead the influence of an interfering colleague: the prime minister's special adviser, Julius Nicholson. The plot involves circulating a false rumour via mobile phones that Julius is lining himself up for foreign secretary in the upcoming cabinet reshuffle. As he carries out this strategy, Tucker moves between Hugh, Ollie and Glenn issuing instructions regarding whom they should call and what they should say. With all members in play, a simultaneous burst of noise and action is created as each sells his lie to a selected media connection. The camerawork and editing rhyme with the pace of this set-up, whipping between the characters to create layers of swift movement and speech. The culmination of these efforts is Tucker's phone call to the prime minister, informing him of Julius's indiscretion and positioning himself as the candidate to demote the special adviser. It is apt that the focus should return ultimately to Tucker, as he has been the central force in the sequence, coordinating the exertions of his colleagues. As he speaks to the prime minister, those colleagues cease their efforts and instead watch in silence, now assuming passive roles, as they become the audience for Tucker's performance.

It is important to note that the synthesis of style and character behaviour in this sequence is based upon an instance of duplicity and malevolence: Julius has ruffled Tucker and he decides to enact his revenge. The sharpness of the camerawork and editing chimes with the harshness of the group's actions as they unquestioningly attack another man's professional reputation. This is a key characteristic of the programme as a whole. As the camera intrudes on characters' space, pulls away from them at will and without warning, or as the editing lacerates their words and deeds, so those characters' fundamental lack of respect or concern for each other is reflected: their psychological disposition is revealed through their manner of depiction. A world is therefore created in which dignity and sincerity have no place and no value. At its centre sits Tucker: the character most at ease within the programme's representational style, most in tune with its frenetic pace and rhythm. Other characters either ride this relentless tide or are consumed by it. Glenn, for example, succumbs to this world as its ruthless hyperactivity reduces him to manic hysteria. In the second of the special episodes that aired between series two and three, he reacts to being usurped by Ollie as Hugh's preferred adviser by launching into a frenzied, rambling tirade against his colleagues. His rage is depicted in the programme's signature frantic style but now, rather than being complicit with that style, Glenn becomes a victim of it: each brutal cut and wild sweep of the camera seeming to emphasise and enhance his anxiety. Within this diatribe, Glenn includes the claim that he is a 'human being', which seems crucial, as he is caught within a representational style that actively dehumanises individuals, and continues to do so even as he voices a need to be recognised humanely. The camera's lack of empathy for Glenn is mirrored in the behaviour of the other characters as his colleagues offer little help: either standing at a distance to him while he spins into turmoil or else, in the case of Terri, attempting to make him shut up. Like Cliff earlier, Glenn finds himself cast adrift from his unforgiving world and, as with Cliff, the representational style that can enrich characters' deviously energetic exploits turns against him and becomes a feature that adds to his victimisation: attacking him as he falls beneath the tide; kicking him while he's down.

Given that the programme's uncompromising style is so closely fused with Tucker's abrasive personality from the very beginning of episode one, the manner in which his eventual downfall is depicted becomes a matter of significance. This occurs within the pivotal sixth episode of the final series, which focuses exclusively on the Goolding Inquiry that has been set up to investigate government leaking, replicating the real-life Leveson Inquiry of 2011 that sought to investigate the practice of phone-hacking. Almost all of the major players from series four give evidence at the inquiry, and the episode departs from the programme's hallmark style to replicate the formal attributes of a televised public inquiry, often resembling the coverage of the Leveson Inquiry itself. In this sense, one naturalistic aesthetic is replaced by another as characters behave spontaneously within a tightly structured series of static shots and an editing pattern that responds rudimentarily to character speech. Whereas *The Thick of It* had previously portrayed its everyday as tense, fast moving and unstable, here there is an effort to emphasise the more mundane, procedural and stifling qualities of political life. This change in aesthetic approach introduces new dramatic and comedic structures to the series, whereby characters are afforded rare time and space to give a considered account of their actions away from the usual frenzied bombardment of events. Naturally, each individual manages to mishandle this opportunity and comes undone as they unsuccessfully attempt to improvise a favourable account of themselves to a scrutinising inquiry panel. In many respects, each of the characters appears no more ludicrous than they had at times in previous episodes, as false perceptions of their own abilities and importance are merely exposed anew in a fresh environment. In this sense, nothing really changes for these characters, as, much like the Leveson Inquiry, little blood is spilt despite the moments of intrigue and occasional humiliation. Even when, in the following episode, Stewart Pearson (the coalition government's director of communications and Tucker's opposite number) loses his job, the grounds for his dismissal have undoubtedly built up over years of incompetent service and are not necessarily related directly to his abysmal jargon-strangled appearance at the inquiry.

For Tucker, however, the change in the programme's style coincides with a dramatic decline in his convictions and status. This doesn't emerge immediately: in his first appearance before the committee, he performs as though holding the belief that his characteristic confidence and acerbic wit will ease him through the proceedings. He treats the process with self-assured disdain and boasts openly about his role in ensuring that details of opposition leader Nicola Murray's disastrous 'quiet bat people' strategy meeting were leaked to the *Daily Mirror* newspaper in a pre-planned photo ambush. Although disconcerted by his blatant disloyalty to his own party's leader, the inquiry committee fail to disrupt Tucker's distorted justification for his actions: he explains that Murray was effectively fair game because she was humiliating his party (in his words, making it look like a calendar featuring dogs wearing dresses and hats). He even concludes his session by overtly leaking the fact that a member of the junior coalition party, Fergus Williams (Geoffrey Streatfeild), who is due to appear next at the inquiry, has been in private talks with the new leader of the opposition, Dan Miller (Tony Gardner), to discuss setting up a future coalition with him. And so Tucker appears unscathed and unmoved by the experience.

However, in his second appearance, that same photo of the Nicola Murray 'quiet bat people' scoop is returned to, with Tucker this time restored in the image (he was originally cropped out in the newspaper story). With magnification, it becomes apparent that he is holding a piece of paper that contains the telephone, NHS and National Insurance numbers of a nurse who had since committed suicide in highly controversial circumstances. The implication is that these details have been obtained illegally and, when he is confronted with this information, Tucker's whole demeanour shifts. His confidence slips away and he loses the vocal fluency that has carried him through series after series of *The Thick of It*. For fifteen seconds he sits in silence, struggling to form any words that might fill the void, before mumbling weakly, 'I don't recall,' and then stumbling again over a series of muffled, awkward and barely formed responses. He is physically uncomfortable – crossing his hands in front of his body, rubbing his mouth and nose – and his answers continue to be stilted and hesitant, littered with long pauses as he struggles to mount a coherent defence of his actions. In all of this, he is framed by the same static camera that does not zoom or pan or pull away from him. He is held in its gaze as each shot is sustained with no sharp edit to provide relief (see page 49). For Tucker, it is as though this new stillness and silence in the programme's editing and framing is stifling: disrupting his natural rhythm and curtailing his habitual manic energy. The sympathetic correlation between aesthetic composition and character behaviour has fallen away as the programme now seeks to isolate Tucker within his world, drawing out his moments of discomposure and offering him neither retreat nor refuge. We realise that the programme's hyperactive naturalistic style had provided Tucker's character with power, facilitating his dexterous manoeuvres and working with him as he carried out his duplicitous schemes. (In previous episodes leading up to the inquiry, it had appeared that power was returning to him: he had successfully removed Nicola Murray from the party leadership and positioned his candidate, Dan Miller, to take over, guaranteeing himself a leading role in that administration.) With this frenetic style discarded, however, and a new mode of fixed scrutiny adopted, the power drains away from Tucker and he is left, finally, humbled. It is telling that his one implied manipulation in the episode, leaking a story about committee member Baroness Sureka (Priyanga Burford), which leads to her temporary removal, takes place off camera and unseen. It is as though the programme has lost interest in his deceptions, not even giving them screen time, and instead adopts a new style to see Tucker in a new light. The inquiry is the fracture point for him within the programme and, in the following episode – the final episode of *The Thick of It* – he is now a victim of its remorseless style as he is rejected by his party and arrested.

One purpose of the inquiry is to discover the truth of events but also, at various points, to emphasise the human cost of individuals' behaviour. Certainly, Tucker is encouraged to consider his actions against Nicola Murray and Mr Tickell (the nurse whose medical records he allegedly accessed) in this light. These two concepts, truth and humanity, evidently do not sit well with him and he is left almost paralysed when he is made to answer for his actions in this way. We might reflect that Tucker's main strength in the programme is to dehumanise situations and also, as a consequence, people. Nicola Murray's career is destroyed because she is a threat to the party institution, and a related character, Ben Swain, is likewise made to face public humiliation because he is no longer of strategic use to Tucker (Swain was part of a chain of historic emails that lead to Murray's removal). We can relate this capacity of Tucker's to the dehumanising quality inherent in the programme's overall stylistic approach to its characters, observable from the very first seconds of episode one in those opening shots depicting Cliff's entrance. With its constant discriminating movement and its abrasive cuts, *The Thick of It* discloses its lack of sustained investment in human emotion. As a consequence, a fictional world is created in which every character is dehumanised to a degree, teetering on the brink of being discarded due to an unforgiving professional logic. Tucker not only enjoys a close affinity with the programme's representational style: his characteristics are woven into the programme's entire fictional world. He sits at its centre, in time with its ruptures and realignments as he negotiates and creates them. No other character displays this kind of ease with the conditions of this world. Fergus and his special adviser, Adam Kenyon (Ben Willbond), engage in equivalent bouts of abuse but often this only reveals their desperation to be seen as powerful: they are not very convincing at it. Other characters such as Peter Mannion and Terri, although at times central to certain political manipulations, often enjoy only a tenuous link to their world and behave as though they would welcome an escape from it (as he nears the end of his political career, Mannion often removes himself from the incessant drive of events, and Terri is literally looking for a way out via redundancy and an early retirement package). Although Stewart Pearson is Tucker's equivalent in an opposite party, he does not share the same capacity for ruthless and vindictive annihilation of careers. It could be said that special advisers such as Phil Smith (Will Smith), Emma Messinger (Olivia Poulet) and Glenn largely respond to events and do not possess Tucker's ability to shape the world around them. All of these characters share certain traits with Tucker – self-preservation, cruelty, insensitivity, manipulation, deception, wit – but none are able to manipulate the conditions of their world to the same degree. Similarly, they are all made victims by the programme's hallmark naturalistic style at various points and none enjoy the kind of close affinity that Tucker attains. Perhaps as a consequence, whilst they are all certainly exposed and humiliated at the inquiry, none suffer the kind of dramatic reversal that Tucker endures.

Which brings us to Ollie Reeder, Tucker's heir apparent in the final moments of the last episode, having replaced him in the senior communications role for the Dan Miller administration. On the one hand, it is unsurprising that Ollie should follow this trajectory. His scruples have been at best questionable throughout the series as he attempted to rise in his career and, although he undoubtedly exaggerates the terms, there is a grain of truth in Glenn's description of him at the inquiry as 'entirely self-serving and spiritually ugly ... a genuinely atrocious person ... a writhing mollusc'. Indeed, the speed with which Ollie steps into Tucker's shoes following the latter's sudden fall from grace is indicative of his disregard for others in the pursuit of his own ambition. Ollie is last glimpsed on screen as he concludes a meeting with some colleagues and ushers them out of the room with a few lines of derogatory banter. At this point, he seems to have stepped into the role with relative ease, casually insulting his peers in the way that Tucker would do regularly as he conducted his morning meetings or descended upon the various government departments. His manner is not as assured as Tucker's, certainly, but we can appreciate that there are the beginnings of a similar approach to the job. However, as Ollie leaves the room and turns a corner, we move to a reverse shot of him smiling to himself gleefully and biting his bottom lip in a private moment of inner elation at the position he now occupies. It is a human response to the situation and entirely understandable given this character's uneven ascent to this position. However, moments of this kind are also out of step with the tenor of the world we have come to know and appreciate in *The Thick of It*. This is a world in which survival has involved an ability to dehumanise, to put distance between oneself and ordinary human emotion. Similarly, it is very unusual for the programme to linger on an individual's sense of joy or satisfaction. Indeed, any intimacy between character and audience usually involves moments of extreme anger or despair. It is possible that Ollie's behaviour marks a new direction for this world, a different way of operating. And yet, he has clearly just tried to emulate Tucker's own abrasive demeanour at the close of his meeting and, furthermore, he is self-conscious enough not to allow this moment of pleasure to be shared with others. These facts suggest that the dynamic has not changed and, more pressingly, Ollie's display of human emotion leaves him vulnerable in a world that does not value humans or emotions. At this point, the camera seems to work *against* Ollie as it captures his expression, betraying his inner feelings to the audience and finding his hubristic weak spot instinctively. If this style of depiction makes Ollie a victim, then it is possible that he has not become like Tucker at all. Rather, we may have come full circle and Ollie instead takes the place of a character like Cliff, destined to be consumed by his world's cruelty.

the thick of it

47

bfi tv classics

the thick of it

bfi tv classics

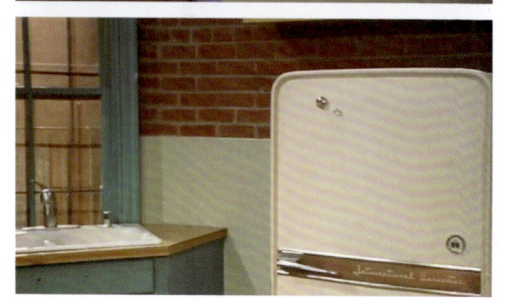

50   *Friends* (1994–2004)

the thick of it

bfi tv classics

the thick of it

bfi tv classics

In the Loop (2009)

3 Words

Hugh Abbott, Minister for Social Affairs, has not been in office for very long before a minor catastrophe befalls him. On his return from a meeting with the prime minister, he informs his special advisers, Glenn Cullen and Ollie Reader, and civil servant Terri Coverley that he has been given the go-ahead to proceed with a new Anti-Benefit Fraud Executive policy. The details of this proposal remain vague but, despite Hugh's inability to remember its precise title and Terri's warnings about spending implications and need for treasury clearance, a decision is made to launch the policy in three stages: an exclusive feature in the *London Evening Standard* newspaper, a lead story on BBC Radio 4's *World at One* programme and an official announcement during a scheduled visit to a Wiltshire primary school. In a rare instance of departmental coordination, the plan comes together and, later that day, Ollie is meeting with the *Evening Standard* journalist in one part of London while Hugh and Glenn listen jubilantly to the Radio 4 broadcast on the radio of the car that takes them to the school. From this moment on, however, the plan begins to unravel.

In the car, Hugh takes a call from Malcolm Tucker. Tucker's tone of questioning is unequivocal as he begins (in reference to the radio broadcast) 'What the fuck was that?' and proceeds to spell out in uncompromising terms why Hugh's announcement has contributed unwittingly to an increasing quantity of profound tensions between the Treasury and government departments. Tucker explains that he will be left to mop up a 'fucking hurricane of piss here from all of these neurotics'. He then moves to a key exchange in the phone conversation:

> TUCKER: What did the prime minister *actually* say to you?
> HUGH: He actually said 'this is exactly the kind of thing we should be doing.'
> TUCKER: *What* did he actually say?
> HUGH: He said 'this is exactly the sort of thing we should be doing.'
> TUCKER: *Should* be doing. *Should* does not mean *yes.*

As Tucker delivers this final revelatory line, we cut to a characteristically intense close-up of Hugh as he clasps his hand to his mouth and looks across at Glenn, mild panic registering in his eyes as new realisation dawns upon him. What follows is a sequence of humiliations as Hugh is made, on Tucker's orders, to bury the initiative entirely. Ultimately, this new strategy forces him to make a major policy announcement at the school that is devoid of any meaningful content whatsoever. The media is subsequently told that the original story was the invention of a 'disgruntled civil servant' and the lack of any coverage in any press agency is treated as a minor success. However, with the Anti-Benefit Fraud Executive policy killed off entirely, there is a further twist to events. In line with the pervading sense of chaos that pulses through the storylines of *The Thick of It*, it emerges that the prime minister has now decided to back the initiative after all. A complete reversal is consequently required and media outlets will be briefed that the announcement did in fact take place (and later that night, Hugh will have to explain, live on radio, that the disgruntled civil servant blamed for inventing the policy was actually the invention of a disgruntled civil servant). Hugh's tentative suggestion that Tucker's snap decision to kill the policy dead was a miscalculation is met with a typically robust response:

> HUGH: We shouldn't really then ... I mean *you* shouldn't have told us to ... should you? (Laughs)

> TUCKER: Don't 'should' me, Hugh. 'Cos I'll 'should' you right back. I'll 'should' you right through that window. None of this *should* be happening, should it? Should it? Should it?
>
> HUGH: ... Is that 'should' in the sense of 'yes?' Or ...?
>
> TUCKER: It's 'should' in the sense of 'you should do as you're fucking told'.

The pivotal role that 'should' occupies in the direction of events offers a brief indication of the special prominence given to words in *The Thick of It*. In both exchanges, Tucker's ability to assume ownership and manipulate the meaning of 'should' allows him to twice direct Hugh's actions: in the first instance by improvising a firm definition to an obviously ambiguous word and, in the second, by reshaping that same word into a threatening verb before forming it into a direct order. In each instance, Tucker's confident employment of even fragments of language contrasts with Hugh's vocal hesitancy and indirectness. The ease with which Tucker encourages Hugh to doubt his understanding of a single-syllable word provides the spin doctor with crucial leverage over the minister, effectively undermining his judgment and reasoning in more profound and wide-ranging ways.

This concentration on the meaning of words also provides a suggestion of the extent to which words are afforded different levels of meaningfulness in *The Thick of It*. The content of the Anti-Benefit Fraud Executive policy is never shared, for example. It can be launched, killed off and relaunched in a manner that suggests the world would be no better or worse if it were to exist or not. Nobody seems able even to remember the name: it is variously referred to as the 'scrounger squad', 'snooper force' and 'sponge avengers' at different points by those responsible for it. In this way, we are given the strong impression that government policy in this fictional environment is essentially meaningless: that descriptions provide only a further level of opaqueness and that the details of any such policy are simply not worth dwelling upon. A hierarchy of language is therefore established whereby the outward-facing statements of government are shown to be inconsequential and ineffectual, whereas, in contrast, the behind-the-scenes verbal interactions between government employees are loaded with weight and force. Tucker uses language as a weapon against Hugh in an almost effortless, straightforward way. Implicitly, he suggests that the minister cannot be trusted with words: cannot be trusted to interpret others' words correctly and, furthermore, cannot be trusted to use words properly – hence the final order that he should do as he's 'fucking told'. It hardly needs to be pointed out that removing Hugh's responsibility for understanding and utilising words essentially strips him of his authority, reducing him to the role of mouthpiece for whatever Tucker – or similar members of the party's senior communications team – approves. In *The Thick of It*, words are power and, as Hugh fumbles over his responses to Tucker in the scenes I've mentioned, he essentially relinquishes power without any struggle, inadvertently highlighting his fallibility with language at the very moment in which Tucker is pointing it out to him with assured vocal eloquence.

The programme returns again and again to situations that play out this close relationship between words and power. As with Hugh's alleged misinterpretation of the word 'should', the connection can often hinge upon small but pivotal phrases. Years later, for example, Nicola Murray – Hugh's departmental successor – makes an error in a policy launch interview when she says that the prime minister is the best 'man' for the job rather than the best 'person', thereby appearing to announce herself as a potential female successor. It emerges that Nicola gave the interview before Tucker had the opportunity to brief her and, again, we are given the impression that ministers cannot really be trusted to deliver messages verbally without the input of a party spin doctor. This, certainly, is a view that Tucker holds and, when Nicola's slip is picked up on by the media as a declaration of political intent, he orders a complete 'lockdown' of all communications within the department. As with Hugh's earlier dilemma, the focus moves swiftly from the content of a potential policy launch to the interpretation of a single misspoken word: from any substance of governance to the minutiae of presentation. As disaster brews, Tucker improvises a series of increasingly erratic media strategies. One of these includes sending Nicola out of the building to make a public statement that she is not intending to stand against the prime minister, before being driven away to a 'pretend' appointment (neatly encapsulating the underlying lack of direction that seems to have gripped events at this stage). Tucker feeds her a series of sentences to deliver, including a declaration that the prime minister is 'the man of the moment'. When Nicola gives her statement, however, she inadvertently changes the meaning of this sentiment entirely by twice saying that he is 'the man, for the moment', thus hinting strongly at his potential impermanence. Tucker has her brought unceremoniously back into the building and points out her error to her: 'There's a huge difference between me saying to you "Nicola, I would like to go *for* a lovely walk with you" and "Nicola, I would like to make a hat out *of* your fucking entrails!"' The result is that he forbids her to deliver her policy speech that evening, thereby averting any further risk but also, crucially, undermining any authority she might otherwise have exerted by suspending her right to speech.

Throughout this chaotic episode, it becomes increasingly clear that Tucker's judgment is, to say the least, off balance. The reason for this is referenced early on in the proceedings. A former spin doctor, Steve Fleming, has returned to the party and has once again forged a close relationship with the prime minister, a fact apparently underlined by Fleming accompanying him on a high-profile 'world tour' in Tucker's place. Although Tucker and Fleming are ostensibly colleagues within the same party, it becomes clear that they are in fact adversaries and, indeed, it emerges that Tucker was responsible for Fleming's forced departure some years ago. Fleming's reappearance is therefore quite clearly a threat to Tucker and, feeling the pressure of this new alignment, he falters visibly. However, in keeping with the programme's insistence upon a relationship between words and power, it is Tucker's vocal eloquence that keeps him afloat. This ability to retain his control and influence through words is emphasised when Terri – correctly, though somewhat foolishly – draws attention to Tucker's expanding catalogue of poor judgment calls from the day's events. Here, Terri appears to have misunderstood that language, in the world of *The Thick of It*, is often direct but is almost never honest for honesty's sake, without agenda, deception or manipulation. As she continues her monologue to Tucker, telling him openly that he is 'wrong like a sultana in a salad', her gathered colleagues – Ollie, Glenn, Nicola and Ben Swain – gradually avert their eyes and visibly back away from her, acknowledging that she has violated dangerously a code of behaviour that exists within their environment. At this stage, Tucker does not respond verbally to Terri's unexpected interjection; instead, Capaldi employs stillness and silence to convey his character's rage, knotting his granite-flesh features together into a dark scowl that conveys Tucker's homicidal regard for Terri. When he does speak, Tucker's voice is low, hoarse and loaded with simmering aggression as he leans in to her and whispers, 'Terri, can we have a word?'

As Tucker leads Terri into a glass-walled adjoining office, we are perhaps expecting him to unleash a characteristic volley of vitriolic abuse. Certainly, Terri walks apprehensively as though she were being led to the gallows. Ollie waves her goodbye in a small, sarcastic gesture loaded with foreboding and finality, and Nicola is heard off camera muttering 'fucking hell' nervously under her breath. At first, expectations of a rage-filled diatribe seem accurate as Tucker's expression remains murderous and he begins by asking Terri, 'How fucking dare you?' But then matters take a different turn as Tucker begins immediately to describe the pressure that is being exerted upon him: 'It feels like my brain has been fucking emptied into little packets, little fucking crisp packets. Cheese and onion fucking crisp packets that contain my living, breathing fucking brain!' He goes on to assert ferociously that the assembled members of the department are stomping on his crisp packets, before pausing and then, extraordinarily, apologising to Terri. There is a shift again as he describes the relative tranquillity of this department compared to Number 10, which is like 'a fucking cancer ward' with people screaming at each other 'you gave me this fucking disease', and he describes being pursued by 'fucking vampire hacks' who want his 'face for a flannel'. With these remarkable thoughts offloaded, Tucker reaches the climax of his speech:

> TUCKER: And you know what? I used to be the fucking Pharaoh, Terri. I used to be the fucking Pharaoh.
> TERRI: Mm.
> TUCKER: Now I'm fucking floundering in a fucking Nile of shit. But I am going to fashion a fucking paddle out of that shit. Yeah?
> TERRI: Mm. Good idea.
> TUCKER: I'm not going down. I am not going down. Yeah?
> TERRI: Yeah.
> TUCKER: (Pause) How're you feeling about things?
> TERRI: Well, you know, I'm just trying to do my best and, you know, make sure I can still get home by six o'clock.

Terri's monosyllabic or mundane responses provide a useful counterpoint to Tucker's grandiose metaphoric descriptions, underlining his ability – and perhaps his need – to employ elaborate language in order to convey his thoughts and feelings. It is ironic that the form in which he describes the innate resourcefulness that will allow him to rise above his current predicament actually highlights his one defining resource: words. Even when reflecting upon the acute pressure and sense of insecurity he experiences, and in a manner that highlights his deteriorating mental health, Tucker manages, instinctively it would seem, to construct strikingly evocative and finely detailed imagery involving his brain in crisp packets, journalist vampires and rivers of shit. Although clearly caught in a moment of crisis, he nevertheless displays the chief characteristic that guarantees power and survival in his world: a fluent command of language. Here, that capacity serves him even at the moment when he is apparently describing his acute mental torment to Terri. He effectively uses words to form a new barrier against her earlier criticisms of him. He takes her appraisal of his failures and intensifies the attack upon himself, leaving her with little choice but to nervously agree with his wild assertions. As a consequence, her questions regarding his flawed professional conduct are never again raised openly and Tucker is able to once more regain his control over events.

In pointing out some of these patterns and structures regarding language in *The Thick of It*, we might also note that it is hardly novel for a situation comedy to exhibit a pronounced investment in the power of words. Indeed, *The Thick of It* is not the first sitcom with a taste for political satire to possess these traits. *Yes, Minister* (1980–4) and *Yes, Prime Minister* (1986–8), for example, are acknowledged starting points for the style and tenor of *The Thick of It*. Indeed, Iannucci's programme was conceived at least partially as a result of its creator's rekindled love for those earlier comedies (Iannucci, 2004). One fairly regular and celebrated feature of both *Yes, Minister* and *Yes, Prime Minister* was the spectacle of cabinet secretary Sir Humphrey Appleby (Nigel Hawthorne) launching into often convoluted and elaborate speeches that relied upon his expert handling of nuanced jargon and bureaucratic language. By the first episode of the final series of *Yes, Prime Minister*, this feature was firmly embedded within the narrative structure, to the extent that a degree of anticipation builds around its inclusion each time. In this particular episode, entitled 'Man Overboard', Sir Humphrey's monologue appears relatively late on in proceedings. Employment minister Stanley Dudley (Michael Byrne) has proposed a seemingly winning strategy to migrate defence operations from the south of England to the north as part of a jobs creation initiative. When raised at a cabinet meeting, it receives the warm approval of the prime minister (Jim Hacker, played by Paul Eddington). Sir Humphrey, however, has previously promised the chief of defence staff that he will block the proposal and has hit upon the strategy of suggesting indirectly to the prime minister that his employment minister is in fact plotting a leadership challenge. The episode then centres upon Sir Humphrey's feeding of this story to Hacker through various means until, finally, the prime minister is convinced that he must turn against Dudley and his proposals. An awkward moment arises when, at the next cabinet meeting, Dudley notices that Hacker's approval of his plan has somehow disappeared from the minutes of the previous meeting. As the prime minister struggles to articulate an answer for this, Sir Humphrey steps in with his own reply to the employment minister:

> It is characteristic of all committee discussions and decisions that every member has a vivid recollection of them and that every member's recollection of them differs violently from every other member's recollection of them. Consequently, we accept the convention that the official decisions are those and only those which have been officially recorded in the minutes by the officials, from which it emerges with an elegant inevitability that any decision that has been officially reached will have been officially recorded in the minutes by the official, and any decision which is not recorded in the minutes has not been officially reached, even if one or more members believe they can recollect it so, in this particular case, if the decision had been officially reached it would have been officially recorded in the minutes by the officials and it isn't, so it wasn't.

Nigel Hawthorne delivers this speech at fast pace in an incessant run of words containing almost no hesitations whatsoever. At its completion, the laughter of the studio audience spills over into applause as the quality of this actor's skilled performance is acknowledged and appreciated. Indeed, the pleasures of this monologue reside not only in its sequence of constructed repetitions but also in Hawthorne's ability to negotiate its intricacies whilst retaining the character's veneer of effortlessness. The extent to which the programme foregrounds the actor's performance in this moment is useful in emphasising the equally assured performance that his character, Sir Humphrey, also gives. Because the monologue contrasts so sharply with the conventional patterns of everyday speech, we cannot help but be aware that it is being manufactured and delivered for a particular purpose. Indeed, it is clearly designed to make the processes of government bureaucracy opaque to the point of incomprehensibility. Although apparently rendered meaningless through its circularity and lack of clarity, the speech succeeds in closing down reasonable, democratic debate. The power of the words is reliant upon a façade of politeness and decorum that frustratingly masks the obvious and serious injustice that is being carried out. It is no surprise that Sir Humphrey's action results in the employment minister resigning from his post: the world that the cabinet secretary has constructed through his choice of language – a world of inflexibility and injustice – can leave no room for any action other than withdrawal if one objects to its terms.

In this instance, the written word and the spoken word carry equal weight, as Sir Humphrey makes clear the impenetrability of the minute-recording process through his equally impenetrable description of it. The scene's deceptive politeness might deceive us into thinking that *Yes, Prime Minister* was defined by this sense of decorum, and therefore somehow safe. The settled nature of the studio location and the clear prompting of studio laughter or even applause may also contribute to this sense, certainly when placed alongside the edgy brutality of *The Thick of It*'s style and tone, for example. But, although there is a veneer of cordiality in this scene, our attention is being drawn very precisely to a dangerous abuse of power. The course of government effectively hinges upon one man's command of the English language, and we can be left in little doubt that Sir Humphrey's efforts, however impressive, are guided by an underlying corruption. Like *The Thick of It*, *Yes, Prime Minister* establishes a clear relationship between an individual's ability with language and the power they wield. And, as with *The Thick of It*, an elected member of parliament is shown to have less power in this respect than those unelected individuals charged with the task of advising them: Hacker does not possess Sir Humphrey's vocal eloquence and needs to have lines written down for him by his cabinet secretary. However, despite its apparently cordial form, the implications of this relationship in *Yes, Prime Minister* are perhaps more serious than *The Thick of It*. Whereas *The Thick of It* deals with ministers at the margins of government (with the Department of Social Affairs and Citizenship regularly referred to as insignificant unless it does something wrong), *Yes, Prime Minister* takes us to the very heart of governance and illustrates with great clarity the extent to which important decisions can be shaped essentially through lies and manipulation. The policy that Sir Humphrey efficiently kills off would have brought employment to the north of England, and no one can find a solid argument against it. And yet it is swept from the cabinet table not through careful debate or strategic argument but through a deceptive use of language. By dealing with the inner circle of government rather than its outer fringes, we might suggest that *Yes, Prime Minister* is equally if not more pessimistic about the potential for corruption in British politics.

Those aspects of self-conscious performance inherent in Sir Humphrey's speech to cabinet find their way into the delivery of lines in *The Thick of It*. In episode two of series three, for example, it emerges that Nicola Murray has inadvertently revealed to a journalist that her department has lost a swathe of crucial immigration data. On hearing this, Tucker suffers a characteristic bout of apoplectic fury and attempts to force the journalist to drop the story via a sequence of barely veiled threats. Later that day, in a moment of relative calm, he calls Nicola to his office at Number 10. Nicola chooses to take Terri with her, presumably to provide a second viable target for his inevitable rage. As the two women enter his office, Tucker sets up proceedings:

> I just wanted to say to you, by way of introductory remarks, that I'm *extremely* miffed about today's events and in my quest to try and make you understand the level of my unhappiness I'm likely to use an awful lot of what we would call violent sexual imagery. And I just wanted to check that neither of you would be terribly offended by that.

Nicola responds by saying, 'I could actually do without the theatrics, Malcolm,' and her brief interjection encapsulates precisely the extent to which Tucker has been introducing his forthcoming tirade to them as a performance replete with certain codes, conventions and styles of language. Tucker's reference to the speech he is about to give furthermore raises the notion of an actor preparing to take on a role that will require a different mode of behaviour and, indeed, language. His sarcastic faux-polite preamble therefore provides them with the equivalent of a theatrical audience warning as the two women literally take their seats in front of him: some viewers may be offended.

Tucker cuts Nicola short and, true to his word, embarks upon a speech that is heavily reliant upon graphic and abusive metaphoric imagery, suspending and stalling any further response that the minister might attempt to formulate:

> Enough. E-fucking-nough. You need to learn to shut your fucking cave, right? Today, you have laid your first big fat egg of solid fuck. You took the data loss media strategy and you ate it with a lump of e-coli and then you sprayed it out of your arse at 300 miles per hour.

The monologue continues at this intensity and, as much as the language is brutal, scatological and graphic, it is also defined by verbal invention and eloquence. Telling Nicola that she has laid her 'first big fat egg of solid fuck' or later that she possesses 'a face like Dot Cotton licking piss off a nettle' displays Tucker's uncompromising and vindictive directness and also reveals his egotistical need to elaborate with words in public, to craft phrases for dramatic and comic impact. So each speech becomes a performance that threatens to turn colleagues into passive audience members. Tucker's behaviour, his chosen method of communication, reveals a need to be not only feared and obeyed but also admired. We are left with the strong sense that he needs his words to be appreciated as much for their comic invention as for their vicious assertion. His use of language discloses an aspect of the character's complex psychology whereby he seeks to abuse others and, at the same time, somehow weirdly entertain them. And so Tucker is always drawn back to elaborate wordplay as a primary means of communication, never able to turn off the kind of performance he describes to Nicola and Terri in this scene.

We might be tempted to say that the directness and relative vulgarity of Tucker's speeches lack the subtlety and finesse of Sir Humphrey's equivalent in *Yes, Prime Minister*. But such an assertion might risk overlooking the extent to which each involves a different kind of subtlety. Unquestionably, Tucker is depicted as a bully, and one who achieves his aims by bullying others relentlessly. However, his impressive and amusing deployment of language makes the act of bullying seductive and intoxicating. It sucks us into the words and invites us – permits us – to laugh at the form the abuse takes. In the scene at Number 10, even Nicola and Terri get inadvertently caught up in the style and content of Tucker's performance. Responding to his demands, Nicola talks hypothetically of going on the BBC's *Question Time* programme wearing a push-up bra and fez in an effort to follow his instructions to the letter from now on. Terri, meanwhile, inadvertently volunteers a reference to 'teabagging', despite no one in the room having mentioned it up to that point. The partial aligning of their words with the tenor of Tucker's underlines the alluring success of his bullying: he achieves his aims through words to such an extent that the victims are actually drawn into the nature of the attacks carried out upon them. Rather than offering any retaliation, they merely fall in with the bully by communicating not only on his terms but also *in* his terms.

In its final series, *The Thick of It* seems to draw more sustained attention to the horror of Tucker's behaviour as it moves towards his eventual downfall. This focus perhaps reaches its climax in the penultimate episode of the final series, which centres entirely upon the Goolding Inquiry into government leaks. At various points in the inquiry, characters are invited to reflect upon the behaviour and conduct of Malcolm Tucker. In one scene, Ollie is reacquainted with some of Tucker's words. A member of the inquiry committee, Simon Weir (Tobias Menzies), raises the question of bullying and asks Ollie directly if Tucker has ever bullied him, to which Ollie responds, 'Do I look like I could be bullied by Mr Tucker?' This rhetorical question is evidently designed to invite a negative answer, yet its asking elicits barely suppressed laughter from the members of the public gallery assembled behind Ollie, causing him to look around as though silently questioning *their* response (see page 49). This moment provides a first slight indication of the disconnect between Ollie's perception of events and their reality, especially as these events relate to his relationship with Tucker. The theme is expanded when Weir begins to read out quotations from a series of civil servants, all of whom claim that Tucker did regularly bully Ollie:

> WEIR: Mr Tucker threatened to remove Mr Reeder's appendix, throw away Mr Reeder and appoint the useless flap of colon as special adviser.
> OLLIE: Yes, well that's ... that's banter.
> WEIR: Mr Tucker told Mr Reeder that he would have him smothered, eviscerated, stuffed, fitted with wheels and donated to an orphanage.
> OLLIE: That's ... what's ... 'cos this is out of context. 'Cos what you don't have there is my reply. So, you know, it's just ...
> WEIR: And what was that?
> OLLIE: Err ... err ... Well, I don't remember what it was on this occasion ... it would have been ... but it would have been, you know, it would have been a zinger, because I gave as good as I got so ... it's not bullying.

What is striking in this exchange is that, even when confronted with Tucker's abuse of him in cold, clear detail, Ollie still maintains that this bullying was in fact 'banter'. Moreover, he suggests that his own capacity for imaginative verbal insult is equal to Tucker's and that it has been unfairly omitted. We see, again, characters being drawn into Tucker's bullying style and, here, rather than object to it as bullying, even at the point when it is plainly and objectively laid out as such, seeking to somehow match that style. Crucially, in attempting to measure up to Tucker, Ollie aspires to replicate his command of words. He understands that words are a definitive power in this world but remains in a state of denial regarding the extent to which he has always been a victim of them. The inclusion of the inquiry's real audience behind Ollie is worth noting, because, self-evidently, they mirror the position of the television viewer as we watch the scene. And, tellingly, they do not recoil in horror at Tucker's inappropriate and offensive use of language. Instead, their laughter continues throughout each of the quotations, their mirth made plain as the camera captures their amused expressions behind Ollie, completing his humiliation. Even as the bullying is framed and laid out as bullying, these individuals with nothing to gain or lose are drawn into Tucker's elaborately brutal and comedic use of language: he does not even need to be in the room to exert that influence.

That 'mirrored' audience at the Goolding Inquiry might give us cause to reflect upon our own relationship to this programme's comedy and, specifically, to a world in which Tucker's bullying style is such a central attraction. *The Thick of It* seems to ask its viewers to examine our own ethical position in relation to the culture of bullying that exists between the characters. Tucker, for example, is an exciting and charismatic force throughout the series. These qualities are perhaps so enticing – both in the writing and in Capaldi's expert performance – that we temporarily suspend certain morals and values we might otherwise hold. As Sam Wollaston, reviewing the first episode of series three for the *Guardian* newspaper, writes:

> I want to work at the Department of Social Affairs and Citizenship. I mean, it's lovely here at the Guardian – looking around, I'm surrounded by intelligent and mostly reasonable people, tapping away on their keyboards. There's some good-natured banter, a few jokes, a bit of gentle

> back-stabbing. But nothing like what goes on in *The Thick of It*. I want the blistering bickering and the bullying, the full-on playground experience, I want to be bollocked by Malcolm Tucker. (Wollaston, 2009)

This light account of the programme's culture of bullying, and its chief antagonist, brings us close to the seductive attraction that a type language which is both funny and abusive can hold. It is hard not to get swept up and perhaps swept away in the manner that Wollaston suggests. Wollaston has to imagine himself in that environment as a victim of Tucker's abuse because that is a condition the programme never inflicts – can never inflict – upon its viewers. We are always safe, always screened-off observers of Tucker's brilliant tirades against a host of apparently incompetent individuals. But that is how bullying works, isn't it? Tolerated by those who are not its victims. Dressed up as humour, more likely to elicit involuntary laughter than moral outrage. By drawing us so effortlessly into Tucker's inventive use of language, perhaps *The Thick of It* asks rather more complex and potentially troubling questions of its audience than might initially be perceived.

Certainly, as the final series reaches its climax, the programme moves to a more overtly critical position in relation to Tucker and his behaviour. *The Thick of It* places its greatest emphasis upon words, rarely dealing with other systems of power such as money, sex or violence. In this way, language – and the ability to use language dexterously – is not simply the characters' livelihood: it is their life. It follows, then, that in order for the programme to finally demonstrate that Tucker has lost his power and influence, it is required to leave him in silence. Our last glimpses of the character, in the final episode, come after he has been arrested and charged for the crime of illegally procuring a member of the public's medical records. Emerging from the police station, Tucker's solicitor stands beside his client and reads out a short prepared statement that protests Tucker's innocence as well as detailing his intention to fight the charges and to step down from top-tier politics for good. After four series filled with chaotic, improvised speech, the bland scripting of the solicitor's announcement provides a structural and tonal contrast of its own. And yet, once it is completed, Tucker appears ready to deviate from the script. Amid the camera-clicks and questions of the assembled press pack, he makes to leave before appearing to change his mind, saying: 'No, I want to say something. I want to say something.' A silence of eight seconds descends, punctuated only by the cameras' rapid-fire bursts, as we move between three separate close-up shots of Tucker's face. And then nothing. He shakes his head, mutters 'It doesn't matter' and is suddenly walking away (see page 49). At this, the journalists lurch into life again, but their actions are futile: Tucker enters a waiting cab that drives him away from the scene. Framed in extreme close-up within the taxi, Tucker exhales and stares blankly into space (see page 49). He does not speak. This is his final act: without words, he has no place in this world. His silence becomes his end.

The Thick of It's utilisation of words as markers of power helps to create a convincing fictional landscape in which language is effectively the primary currency. More than that, however, it builds upon themes raised in earlier programmes like *Yes, Minister* and *Yes, Prime Minister* by providing a stark warning against the manipulation of the political system. The programme puts forward the implicit case that, if the convictions and morals of the political class are so wafer thin that a Malcolm Tucker (or, indeed, a Sir Humphrey Appleby) can rip them apart so easily, the establishment has failed and the system courts corruption. The programme presents a fictional world that is ruled by words alone, governed by those whose verbal eloquence places them in control. The consequent suggestion is that, behind those words, there is a moral vacuum, a profound absence of sincerity or virtue. It might be said that programmes like *The Thick of It* and *Yes, Prime Minister* are inherently cynical about the systems they portray, given that they portray those systems as inherently cynical. But it seems more the case that they warn against cynicism, precisely by demonstrating where cynicism can lead a political system. Tucker, and Sir Humphrey before him, does not seem to believe in anything, and so perhaps it should be shocking to us how easily he is able to attract followers and gain influence through his words alone.

It is perhaps inevitable that, within *The Thick of It*'s skewed hierarchy, some voices fail to be heard. Episode five of series four, for example, involves a rare case of a government policy being designed and implemented to benefit a section of society. Junior coalition partner MP Fergus Williams and his special adviser, Adam Kenyon, have designed a new 'carer's pass' that entitles young carers to free public transport. Two such carers have been invited into the department to launch the policy. Throughout the day, this policy and the young carers recede further and further into the background as Fergus and Adam endeavour to safeguard their future political careers. In this final series of *The Thick of It*, these two men come to represent the extent to which the culture of abusive vocal humour has permeated this Westminster environment. They litter their conversations with expletives and graphic imagery that clearly aspire to the level of offensive eloquence a character like Tucker achieves. And so, in this episode, when they have apparently smeared the reputation of their senior coalition partner MP, Peter Mannion, they celebrate in the following way:

> FERGUS: You know what you've done?
> ADAM: Yeah?
> FERGUS: You have bought a fan. You plugged it in. You turned it on. You turned the dial up to maximum ...
> ADAM: It wasn't a weak fan. It wasn't one of those office fans. It was a Dyson. And I stood the other side of it ...
> FERGUS: ... Did a liquid shit on it ...
> ADAM: ... Trousers down ...
> FERGUS: And where did the shit go? All over Mannion.

The scatological nature of this metaphoric description bears the hallmarks of Tucker's language, as it in fact resembles directly the speech he made to Nicola Murray about her eating his media strategy with a 'lump of e-coli' and spraying it out of her arse. And yet, perhaps because it is two of them, perhaps because their vocal intonations and physical gestures do not carry the same manic violence of Tucker's, it is the case that their attempts at that style of communication never quite ring true. Indeed, they come to be rather desperate figures: desperate to be taken seriously and rise above their diminished status as junior members of the coalition government. It is telling that, in an effort to achieve this status, they seek to emulate a style of vocal delivery rather than any set of values or principles. In this way, although their aims are never fulfilled, Fergus and Adam at least possess an acute awareness of how hierarchies function in their world and how they might use words to attain power.

It is certainly the case that neither of these men are invested in the young carers they have invited into the department to launch their policy. Adam suggests killing off the launch altogether until Fergus reminds him of its cosmetic value to the party faithful. In the end, the two young people are made to effectively front the policy announcement as an afterthought, captured appropriately in the final minute of the episode as the credits roll. Fergus and Adam abandon them and, as the last credit fills the screen, we hear on the soundtrack the voice of the female young carer, Rohinka (Mandeep Dhillon): '… so this carer's pass is … is … is a blessing really …' The image fades to black and the episode ends. The marginalisation of Rohinka's voice provides a fleeting but poignant climax to the day's events. Her willingness to endorse Fergus and Adam's policy despite their mistreatment of her is noble and her candid honesty, exemplified by her slightly faltering delivery, contrasts significantly with the shallow vindictiveness of their behaviour. In the rarest and briefest of moments, someone in the world of *The Thick of It* speaks honestly and openly about something that matters. It lasts four seconds. We might conclude that this treatment amounts to one of the programme's most direct and striking criticisms of its central characters: the brevity comes to symbolise their disregard for the people they are employed to represent and serve. *The Thick of It* gives us a world in which words can buy power, yet that power is only ever used for self-advancement or even self-preservation. This world of words is entirely inward-looking, solipsistic, bound up in itself, obsessed with its own cruel inventiveness: adrift almost entirely from the world outside and around it. It stands to reason, then, that when a young woman bravely stands up to talk about her personal sacrifice and the profound difference even free public transport could make to her life, nobody listens. Her words simply have no value to anyone in this world.

4 Spaces

As part of an extended consideration of spaces and meanings in films, Deborah Thomas poses a series of initial, framing questions:

> What sorts of geographical and architectural spaces seem to be significant in these films? How are these spaces structured and how do they relate to one another: are they seen as similar or as contrasting or as both? What sorts of characters are well-suited to inhabit them, and which are ill at ease? How do the spaces and their treatments relate to the thematic concerns of these films? (Thomas, 2001, p. 10)

We might take these guiding notions as useful starting points when thinking about the spaces presented in *The Thick of It* and, indeed, a number of comparable television programmes. Thomas's points move beyond questions of whether spaces on screen are simply coherent or authentic – whether we can navigate them and believe in them as real locations – to place an emphasis upon the expressive potential of those spaces. In this sense, the design and arrangement of spaces in film and television not only underpin the 'thematic concerns' of the work by providing an environment in which those concerns can be played out and realised. Rather, the way in which spaces are designed and arranged can also successfully foreground those concerns, to the extent that spaces become significant or pivotal elements in a film or television programme's dramatic aims.

Part of this significance derives from the capacity for television spaces to convey a particular tone and mood. Karen Lury has drawn attention to the ways in which situation comedies had conventionally relied upon a limited number of locations, centring most usually on the domestic living room (Lury, 2005, p. 157). When sitcoms were almost always filmed on studio sets, there were clearly practical and financial reasons for limiting the range in this way, and the shared living room perhaps provides a useful space in which different cast members can plausibly enter, interact and leave throughout an episode. As Lury explains:

> Other sets are used (often a kitchen and one or more bedrooms), but the outside world rarely appears. Therefore, the sitcom is, characteristically, a closed set and the position of characters within their environment quickly becomes established and remains fixed for the entire series. (Ibid.)

We can appreciate that this perpetual return to an established location provides an orientating function by allowing the viewer to very quickly familiarise themselves with a space and its inhabitants. However, it is also the case that this closing off from the outside world and limiting characters to a shared environment also has the effect of confining those individuals by drawing them together in – often – close proximity.

In some programmes, this proximity engenders a composition of intimacy, affection or support. In *Friends* (1994–2004), for example, there is a strong sense that no matter how dysfunctional the characters' lives became in the world 'outside', they would always find comfort and security in the central location of a shared apartment (shared between the six central protagonists, regardless of legal tenancy). It is therefore both striking and entirely logical that, in the final scene of the final episode, the characters spend time in that space, even when it is emptied of all personal possessions, and take an extended moment to reflect collectively upon its qualities: the meanings it holds for them. And, once they have left (retreating together to their other safe-haven space of the Central Perk coffee house), the barren apartment is captured yet again in a slow, lingering panning shot that is underscored by a sentimental acoustic guitar melody (see page 50). These are the very final moments of *Friends* before the end credits, the last images of that fictional world that viewers of the programme will ever see. The sequence certainly possesses an appropriately mournful tone as it depicts the space suddenly bereft of its erstwhile inhabitants. At the same time, the centrality of this space within the programme's narrative is made explicit as we are presented with a warm, nostalgic last look at it. The last thing we say 'goodbye' to is the apartment itself. The close fusion of character to space is emphasised in this sequence, underlining the fact that locations in sitcoms often function as far more than simply places to facilitate interaction. And of course, due in part to the conventions of studio-based television sitcoms, the apartment removes and even shields the characters from the outside world. It is somewhat ironic that the end credits of this final *Friends* episode are laid over a montage of New York scenes. As we are presented with these images of city skylines, night-time streets and neon signs, we are surely reminded of how little exterior scenes of this kind have featured in the lives of the programme's characters and how insignificant the reality of New York living has been to any of the friends. They are simply cocooned away from it for the most part and, whilst the shared apartment exists as a symbol of their shared existence among each other, its interior becomes equally symbolic of their group interiority. A central tension of the final episode lies perhaps in the fact that this group of adults have grown up together yet, spatially and psychologically, have never been fully required to go out into the world. As they make their way to the familiar Central Perk coffee house – a straightforward substitute for the space of the apartment – we might question whether, even now, they are entirely ready to make that journey.

  In *Friends*, the space of the apartment therefore becomes a haven for characters, allowing them to alleviate, suspend or even delay some consequential pressures of adult life. Spaces in television comedies do not always offer this kind of security or comfort, however. *The Office*, for example, represents perhaps the most carefully realised effort to make a location realistically banal, unsociable and even oppressive.

The programme revels in the dehumanising potential of a drab, open-plan workplace, and its characters become unavoidably entwined with their environment as their thoughts and words are seemingly stifled amid the functional tedium of the office. The extent to which two characters, Tim (Martin Freeman) and Dawn (Lucy Davis), may or may not manage to resist this acquiescence to the mundane becomes a central dramatic theme within the programme's narrative as both are aware of what they risk becoming, and each tentatively desires a life away from the office where they can be together. We might reflect, however, that they are surrounded by workers for whom that struggle has already ended, if it took place at all. These background figures have become featureless human furniture within the colourless, fluorescent-lit vacuum of their workplace. They consequently represent the normal rhythm of working life in *The Office*, whereas a resistance to it defines Tim and Dawn. The stifling bleakness of the programme's location threatens to become problematic when, in the final episode, Tim and Dawn's narrative is at long last afforded a positive resolution as they begin a romantic life together, yet events still unfold in the office that has entrapped them previously: they are still bound to that space. This tension between escape and entrapment is resolved efficiently, however, as the space is visibly transformed through the convention of the Christmas office party.

In this final episode, the festive event seems to take on aspects of the carnivalesque, where certain rules and conventions are temporarily suspended or reversed. So Dawn and Tim's romantic union is permitted, and makes sense in the newly altered environment. Equally, boss-from-hell David Brent (Ricky Gervais) is allowed the possibility of a romantic future as his blind date for the evening encourages him to see his life in a new, more positive light, so much so that he finds the confidence to tell long-time office bully, Chris Finch (Ralph Ineson), to 'fuck off'. More generally, the behaviour of other 'background' office workers is, for that evening, changed as they abandon the routine confines of their working environment to talk, laugh, dance and drink together. Unlike the final episode of *Friends*, which offered its characters the opportunity

The Office (2001-3)

to reflect upon the unifying and endearing qualities of their shared apartment space by making them say goodbye to it, *The Office* allows its characters to re-engage with their otherwise stiflingly banal workplace by reinventing it as an arena for revelry, self-discovery and romantic union. In doing so, it provides them with a temporary reprieve from their everyday surroundings precisely by changing the form and tone of those surroundings. In this way, the series' ultimately upbeat ending is rooted strongly in a dramatic change to the physical environment. However, this happiness is not unqualified, as we can only acknowledge that the festivities of the Christmas party are but a temporary reprieve according to the conventions of the carnival. On the following day, inevitably, the office will return to its habitual state and its occupants will again become confined to a claustrophobic and dreary reality.

Whereas *Friends* and *The Office* create spaces that enclose characters hermetically to varying degrees and in contrasting ways (by cushioning them *from* a potentially stark reality in the first instance or by trapping them *within* a stark reality in the second), *The Thick of It* allows sets of shared tonal characteristics to expand and take shape across a range of different spaces, unifying these locations within an encompassing fictional world. In this way, spaces are structured according to a series of overarching thematic concerns, along the lines that Deborah Thomas suggests in relation to film at the beginning of this chapter. Locations in *The Thick of It* have attributes in common that are bleak, impersonal, repressive and uncomfortable. Some of these qualities might remind us of the atmosphere presented in the workplace of *The Office*, but, unlike that programme, those characteristics are not contained only within a work environment – a depiction that carries the implied notion of more accommodating and sympathetic environments elsewhere. Rather, *The Thick of It* presents a world in which every room, every building, every exterior is laden with the same stifling anxiety, leaving characters trapped within an ever-expanding matrix of hardships and hopelessness. Although not office-based exclusively, these elements are emphasised strongly within the programme's office environments. These interiors possess a fundamental lack of privacy as individual characters are rarely afforded any time to reflect or regroup before another imposition brings with it a fresh assortment of tortuous dilemmas. In the first series and part of series two, for example, the warren-like offices of the Department of Social Affairs allow for unscheduled and unanticipated intrusions from an array of different characters through various entrances. And so, as the minister, Hugh Abbott, attempts to strategise with his special advisers, Ollie and Glen, he is frequently stalled by the arrival of characters ranging from Dan Miller to Julius Nicholson to Terri Coverley to, inevitably, Malcolm Tucker. The impression is given of Hugh as a man besieged by uninvited (and frequently unwelcome) guests as his private room is treated effectively as a public thoroughfare. Although Hugh's office, and offices like his, have apparently clear boundaries that might require access to be requested, it nevertheless bears all the wretched hallmarks of an open-plan office design – the elemental source of slow-burning torment in *The Office*. Each new invasion into Hugh's space therefore emphasises and extends an intrinsic lack of respect afforded to ministers in *The Thick of It*, serving to undermine any elevated status he might otherwise have aspired to.

The programme moves beyond the conventional portrait of professional spaces as demoralising and inhospitable, however, as this inherent lack of dignity and respect within the workplace escalates into moments of vitriolic antagonism. In the third episode of the first series, for example, Hugh is attempting to undertake what is intended to be a benign interview-based piece with journalist Angela Heaney (Lucinda Raikes). This meeting has already developed into something of an ambush. Angela does not pose the kind of gentle questions about a recent housing bill success that Hugh had rehearsed earlier with Glen and instead pursues the mounting scandal of the minister's second property in London, which he does not occupy but is apparently unwilling to sell. Taking place in a glass-walled room, this becomes both an intensely private and uncomfortably public ordeal as Hugh is trapped in the space with Angela and, at the same time, his awkwardly defensive demeanour can be easily observed by anyone looking in (and, indeed, Terri often hovers in the background of the shot, peering uselessly into their glass enclosure). We cut between this interview to scenes of Tucker first learning of its significance and then charging manically towards Hugh's location, shoving colleagues out of his path and yelling 'Where the fuck is he?' when he enters the department. As the interview with Angela reaches a particularly difficult stage, with Hugh falteringly refuting the implicit accusation that he is a racist for not selling his empty second home to an Asian family, Tucker arrives in the corner of the frame, his body slamming audibly against the glass partition wall as he reaches his destination. The camera remains behind Hugh to frame Tucker through the glass as he stalks around outside the interview room. His demeanour is both menacing and physically intrusive, distracting Hugh and disrupting any vocal fluency he might have hoped to achieve in his responses to Angela. Tucker moves to the glass pane directly in front of Hugh, behind Angela, places his hands on the surface and motions with his head for Hugh to step outside the room. Hugh misreads this signal, saying that Tucker is 'mucking about' and attempts to continue the interview. At this, Tucker marches around the office to the door, knocking redundantly as he swings it open and asks, in strained tones, to 'borrow the minister for a second'. This action clearly continues a pattern within *The Thick of It* of individuals having their private space intruded upon unceremoniously and without warning. Events intensify, however, as Tucker leads Hugh out of the office, positions him in a space behind where Angela is seated, and proceeds to abuse him verbally (see page 51). We remain in the room with Angela and, although the glass muffles the sound of Tucker's invective, key phrases such as 'stupid cunt' are made audible as his voice reaches crescendo.

As Angela turns around to witness Tucker's assault beyond the glass, the demeaning nature of *The Thick of It*'s work environment is made emphatic. Clearly, no effort is made to preserve Hugh's dignity here and, indeed, his private humiliation is made unavoidably public within this structured office space. Terri makes an inexpert attempt to divert Angela's attention away from the abusive spectacle by entering the room to interject with offers of more coffee and tea. In doing so, she actually manages to amplify Tucker's tirade by leaving open a door that had previously buffered at least some of the audio detail, and so her polite interjection is undermined entirely as it coincides with Tucker – now suddenly louder – exclaiming 'You're a fucking prick!' As Terri speaks, Tucker and Hugh are once again framed in the background and the contrast between her forced attempt at casualness and Tucker's fierce diatribe creates the accurate impression that brutality is unremarkable within this workplace. Indeed, the use of a glass office in this instance unites the attempted decorum of the interior (Hugh's awkward interview, Terri's refreshment reconnaissance) with the unbridled malice of the exterior space. When he re-enters the room having been dismissed by Tucker, Hugh is unable to gloss over the reality of the working environment that Angela has just witnessed. He merely asks her if she could hear any of what had been said, adding weakly that 'we can be quite brutal to each other … because we're actually very, very good friends …', despite all evidence to the contrary.

It makes sense that Tucker should become synonymous with the intrusive nature of the programme's work environments, given that he often exists at the epicentre of *The Thick of It*'s brutalised fictional world. Indeed, when, in the second series, the department moves to new and almost fully open-plan premises replete with shared spaces and a plethora of glass partitions, he intensifies his invasive approach with enthusiasm and energy. He apparently makes a point of descending upon colleagues without warning and delivering verbal tirades in public, often to impromptu audiences of fellow workers. At one point in the third episode of series two, for example, Ollie, Terri and Robyn (Polly Kemp) are gathered on a stairwell landing overlooking the vast expanse of the lobby, discussing the location's merits as a suicide spot. The conversation encapsulates succinctly the tone and mood created within this work environment, but their speculations are cut short as, looking up from the ground floor, Tucker spots the group and yells menacingly at them to 'get back to work'. The space therefore works with Tucker in this moment and others to make him ever more incessant and inescapable, allowing him to invade the space of others with almost omniscient freedom. And yet, at one stage, even he becomes victim to this ruthless blending of the private and the public within *The Thick of It*'s work environments.

In the seventh episode of series three, Tucker faces the prospect of being evicted from his professional world permanently as his occasional nemesis within the party, Steve Fleming, orchestrates a forced resignation. Fleming leads Tucker into his office to deliver this news, the relatively confined interior complementing the spiteful intensity that exists between these two men: Tucker's characteristic aggression met by Fleming's patronising show of obsequiousness. This tension is broken, however, as first Julius Nicholson and then Nicola Murray blunder into the room, turning Fleming's moment of private vindictiveness into a public fall from grace for Tucker. As his space is now intruded upon, Tucker begins to suffer the lack of dignity he ordinarily inflicts upon others. In keeping with the overall arrangement of office spaces in *The Thick of It*, the assault can come from all directions unexpectedly and, in this scene, Nicola is unwilling to provide any assistance to Tucker, whilst Julius is merely revelling in the schadenfreude of his now former colleague's discomfort, leaving Tucker both trapped and isolated. The onslaught is complete when Fleming draws Tucker's attention to a television set behind him that displays the news story 'Malcolm Tucker resigns'. This places his forced departure in the most public sphere and extends the notion that he is under attack from all angles: not only the uninvited interlopers before him in Fleming's office but also the whole national media, represented in the television set behind him. This ambush motif is mirrored when, moments later, Tucker enters his own office to find his personal assistant Sam (Samantha Harrington) visibly upset as a group of government officials surround her in a somewhat threatening manner. His concern for her on discovering this scene is indicative of the strong and, for this programme, unusual loyalty that endures between these two characters. He tells them to 'leave her fucking alone', reassuring her as he tells her to go. Tucker follows his own advice to take flight and, in scenes intercut with the episode's end titles, marauds through the corridors and offices, yelling abuse at Fleming and pushing Julius violently up against a wall. This new mobility can be read as Tucker's attempt to regain authority even at the point where he should exert the least influence: if he reclaims these spaces, he clings to power. And so, even as he finally strides out towards the exit, he fills the interior with movement and noise, whirling around to shout: 'You will see me again,' and repeating: 'You will fucking see me again' as he stalks away (see page 51).

Instances of this kind effectively depict the office environments of *The Thick of It* as emotionally bleak and bereft of human compassion. Such features would correspond with the highly critical stance adopted by the programme in relation to the institutions of government, so that these characteristics become synonymous with the headquarters of political power. As we move beyond those zones, however, such traits endure. When characters are presented with the opportunity to escape the confines of their immediate workplace, they find their surroundings no less accommodating or comfortable. We might expect that events such as a team-building awayday – represented in episode three of series four as Stewart Pearson's weekend 'thought camp' at a Kent hotel – could retain traces of the characters' oppressive work environment. And, indeed, although the shackles of ordinary working life are notionally thrown off, Stewart's sessions simply form themselves into a new kind of prolonged ordeal. For the attending minister, Peter Mannion, the day is made especially humiliating as his reluctance to partake in the abstract team-building exercises results in a recent media disaster of his being projected in a PowerPoint display to the group, and he is made to play a game where he has to guess the word 'inclusivity' – a concept that is almost incomprehensible to Peter – Post-it-noted to his forehead. And so, like the offices and corridors of government buildings, the interior location of the awayday is made uncomfortable and intrusive for the minister. Even escaping to the hotel gardens brings further distress when a member of the public photographs both Peter and Stewart as they balance on children's play equipment in an attempt to gain a mobile phone signal. The photograph goes viral, causing both Peter and Stewart acute humiliation.

So perhaps we should not be surprised that an 'awayday' setting offers no respite for the characters. It might be anticipated that transplanting the work environment to a country hotel would simply relocate a series of underlying tensions and tribulations. However, it is also the case that every outside location that the characters visit seems imbued with invasive, claustrophobic and demeaning qualities. In the first episode of the second series, Hugh visits a factory and is accosted immediately by a disgruntled woman who demands to know whether he has ever experienced clearing up his own mother's piss, as she has with her mother. This encroachment, recorded by the attending press corps, sets the tone for the visit as Hugh walks through cavernous industrial spaces, his awkward interactions with his guides drawn out painfully as Robyn misreads his signals to leave and instead extends their stay. Finally, he seeks refuge with Glenn in a vacuous and dimly lit abandoned office within the factory site, its stark lifelessness exemplifying the bleak tenor of the time spent away from the office (see page 51). In this space, Hugh voices his deep-rooted hatred of the 'actual people' (members of the public) who have pursued him that day, before attempting to deal with the negative publicity his visit has attracted as a result of the aggrieved woman's earlier interruption. Consequently, rather than offering an escape from the traumatic environment of the government offices, the factory becomes another kind of trap for Hugh as he faces equivalent onslaughts from new and unanticipated directions.

Given the oppressive nature of spaces in *The Thick of It*, it seems especially apt that Hugh's successor, Nicola Murray, should suffer from mild claustrophobia, as though she were responding viscerally to a world that closes in around its occupants. Her condition is revealed in the first episode of the third series when, on her first day in the job, she is reluctant to enter a lift with Tucker. In typically insensitive fashion, he labels her 'fucking mental' when she explains her phobia to him. Nicola's claustrophobia returns in subsequent episodes, combining with a general anxious disposition that seizes her regularly. This pattern continues when, incredibly, Nicola becomes leader of the opposition, and reaches its zenith in the fourth episode of series four when, on a Bradford-bound train journey intended to launch a 'listening' tour of the United Kingdom, she becomes overwhelmed by threats to her leadership. Her sense of entrapment was already taking shape when, once she has concluded a brief interview with Sky News on the train, it becomes clear that hapless press officer John Duggan (Miles Jupp) has inexplicably arranged for the reporter and cameraman to remain in the seats opposite Nicola for the duration of the journey. As a consequence, they will be observing her every move as she attempts to conduct the day's business with her special adviser, Helen Hatley (Rebecca Gethings). Meanwhile, at party headquarters, Tucker is working to manoeuvre Nicola out of office and he begins by persuading Ben Swain to resign in order to trigger a leadership crisis. Back on the train, Nicola and Helen receive news of this planned betrayal but, in the immediate presence of the Sky reporters, are forced to suppress their reactions to it. The acute tension of this moment is enhanced due to the careful choice of a particularly restrictive location; the seating on the train is frustratingly confining but, at the same time, uncomfortably borderless. In keeping with the programme's overall structuring of spaces, the environment around Nicola and Helen works against them, intensifying the pressure they experience in an already precarious situation.

Nicola and Helen leave their seats in order to escape the glare of the reporters, adjourning to a vestibule between carriages. The two women remain in this space as the episode alternates between their attempts to manage the situation and Tucker's efforts to exacerbate the crisis (either personally or via Ollie, who plays a role in the leadership coup from his hospital bed following appendix surgery). Although intended as a site of temporary refuge, the vestibule offers little respite for Nicola and Helen. As Tucker steadily increases the pressure on Nicola, her behaviour becomes increasingly erratic and panic-stricken. She attempts to placate Ben by offering him shadow chancellor; she tries to plan a reshuffle as Helen takes notes on a railway emergency instruction card; when John Duggan interrupts them, she shrieks at him to go away and stop 'molesting' them; and, finally, she allows Tucker to persuade her to give an impulsive interview to the Sky News team on the train. These lapses in rational judgment and behaviour coincide with Nicola's sense of entrapment in the train vestibule, a notion that is enhanced as she is frequently framed within its tight, restrictive structure (see page 52). She is out of breath and flustered as she speaks, indicating an attack of claustrophobia, and paces around the space as though she were a trapped prisoner. Nicola's apparent sensation of the walls closing in around her coincides with Tucker's relentless efforts to manoeuvre her into a tight corner from which she cannot return. Again, *The Thick of It* finds ways of making a seemingly innocuous space work against its characters, amplifying their feelings of entrapment and persecution. It is perhaps easy, given the tempestuous swirl of events, to overlook the fact that this train journey was intended to mark a break from the pressures of leadership that Nicola had been experiencing, and to set out a new policy direction for her. In this fictional world, however, such options are inevitably not made available to characters and, instead, the train interior simply becomes yet another repressive environment. Ultimately, Nicola cannot withstand that level of intensity and elects to leave the train altogether, because she is 'hyper-fucking-ventilating'.

In contrast to Tucker's exit after Steve Fleming unceremoniously sacks him, Nicola is unable to take command of her surroundings as a means of regaining control of a situation. Instead, she accepts that she is incapable of withstanding these conditions and flees without defiance. As she hurries away from the train, desperately attempting to solicit support from her cabinet colleagues in various breathless phone calls, Nicola retreats rather than advances. She recoils not only from the airless, cramped train carriages that induced her claustrophobia but also from the political manoeuvres that have her cornered: the two have become intertwined now. In these moments, even before it emerges that statements made in her second Sky News interview will ultimately lead to her resignation, it becomes clear that Nicola is fundamentally ill-equipped to cope with the rigours of her world. Furthermore, it is equally apparent that these pressures can erupt in any location within this fictional world: like Hugh before her, Nicola finds that any temporary reprieve from the tumult of the immediate workplace environment provides no respite from its tensions.

It may be the case that occasions such as factory visits, awaydays and campaign train journeys provide only the illusion of a relief from the workplace for characters in *The Thick of It*, a notion punctured swiftly as the locations for these events rapidly take on a set of characteristics resembling closely those found in the government offices. However, if this is so, we might equally expect that the private personal spaces of characters – their homes, for example – could at least offer some kind of refuge. It would be perhaps unrealistic to suppose that a space resembling the cocoon-like ambience of the shared apartment in *Friends* might exist in the world of *The Thick of It*, given the starkly different dramatic and comedic tones of the two programmes. However, as a far more direct comparison, *Yes, Prime Minister* provides a prototype for how a politician's – or, indeed, prime minister's – home life might compare with their professional existence. Although Prime Minister Jim Hacker can often be subject to gently barbed conjecture from his wife, Annie (Diana Hoddinott), an underlying and consistent warmth exists between the characters, effectively preserving a comfortable status quo of mutual support. This notion of comfort extends to the *mise en scène* of the Number 10 Downing Street flat they occupy, with its soft furnishings and easy chairs contrasting markedly with the more functional lines of the desks and office furniture found in the professional zones within that same address.

As a result, although government business is often discussed in the Hacker home and many guests arrive to debate such matters, these exchanges take place in a cordial and relaxed domestic environment. We might read Annie's apparent refusal to take Jim's occupation too seriously, as she perceptively highlights the various hypocrisies of government or neatly curtails her husband's pompous oratory vignettes, as confirmation that she offers a life outside political office for him. Annie will not allow him to become defined by his job title and, in many ways, provides an essential balance in his life. If his political career ended tomorrow, their life would continue together. In short, he is needed and loved.

Given the thematic similarities between the programmes, we might compare this portrait of the domestic in *Yes, Prime Minister* with depictions found in *The Thick of It*. The homes of characters are occasionally glimpsed in *The Thick of It* but, in contrast to most situation comedies, are not given significant narrative prominence. Moreover, ministers generally refer to their domestic life in

bfi tv classics

Yes, Prime Minister (1986–8)

negative terms: one of Nicola's fears is that, were she to divorce her psychologically abusive husband, she would be left with custody of their increasingly dysfunctional children; on one occasion, Hugh is unable to stay in his Westminster flat because his wife overreacts to their daughter's phantom ear infection and makes him drive twenty miles through the night so that he can sit uselessly at her bedside. These figures – the ministers' respective spouses and children – are always an off-screen presence, an invisible backdrop to on-screen events that, at times, can add yet another layer of pressure and anxiety. On the one occasion we see Hugh's home, in the second episode of the first series, he sits alone at his kitchen table in the middle of the night. The smoke from his lighted cigarette drifts through the dusk as he hunches over a mug of coffee (see page 53).

This portrait of exhausted seclusion intensifies as he takes a call from Terri and explains that he has only just been dropped back home from work and is due to be picked up again in three hours: 'I didn't think it was worth taking my trousers off.' Terri, inevitably, has bad news regarding a negative story about Hugh that is due to run in the press but he cuts her off because he has 'an egg on'. Hugh's lack of sleep, his dependence on caffeine and nicotine, the lonely gloom of the kitchen and even the pathetic sustenance of the single boiled egg combine to form a bleak illustration of his domestic existence. Tonally, there is very little to distinguish this dreary scene from one set within the government offices, certainly nothing approaching the contrast between work and home found in *Yes, Prime Minister*. Hugh's home is empty, silent and cold. He is as isolated emotionally here as he would be in his office and, when Terri rings, the kitchen becomes just another workspace, prone to the kinds of interruptions and intrusions that are hallmarks of professional life in *The Thick of It*.

Uncompromising depictions of domestic life persist in *The Thick of It*. The lack of personal privacy in flat-shares, for example, is explored as Emma and Phil live together inharmoniously. The communal space of the sitting room becomes an arena for these tensions to be explored as Phil, Emma and Ollie (when he and Emma are dating) engage in shifting cycles of mutual animosity. The blurred territorial lines of the shared setting become a source of conflict between Phil and Ollie particularly, which might lead us to suggest that they are engaged in an unspoken rivalry for Emma's affections. Perhaps, but when Ollie and Emma are afforded a rare moment of privacy in the flat (during the fifth episode of series three), we find them on the verge of ending their relationship. As a consequence, they are awkward and uptight together as they enact a bitter reversal of loving union. The couple's interaction with their domestic space provides a visual illustration of these tensions. They are seated at a dining table but Ollie has failed to prepare dinner and now inexpertly hacks at an array of vegetables he has stolen from Phil. Emma, meanwhile, taps away at her laptop keyboard and, when Ollie attempts to inject a 'sexier' mood by switching off a standard lamp behind her, she complains that she needs the light to work. When we return to this scene, Ollie has clearly attempted to remedy the evening by ordering a takeaway curry and Emma does close the lid of her laptop but then switches on the radio behind him so that she can listen to their respective bosses, Nicola and Peter, appearing on BBC Radio 5 Live. We might recognise the familiar intrusion of work into the home, echoing the phone call Hugh receives from Terri. This version of that trend is perhaps more brutal, however, as Emma elects to bring the two together. It is possible to feel sympathy for Ollie in this situation, as he momentarily mistakes Emma's move towards the radio for a romantic advance towards him. But he resists this kind of sentimentality as he cynically responds to Emma's hostility, asking at one stage: 'You know, when your mum walked out ... do you think that maybe wasn't just about your dad?' The shared leisure time at home offers no positive enjoyment for either character and, instead, becomes an awkward and unpleasant ordeal. In this dining room, as in Hugh's kitchen, work might as well invade the space, because domestic life is depicted as equally strained and uncomfortable. In this way, the home offers no respite from the intolerable burden of work. In tone and mood, the two environments are almost indistinguishable. It is no surprise, then, that when we first enter Malcolm Tucker's home, in episode seven of series three, it is because he has invited a group of journalists there in an attempt to positively influence their opinion of him (and turn them against his in-party rival, Steve Fleming). We might suggest that

Tucker's centrality within the fictional world of *The Thick of It* allows him to embrace its fusion of work and domestic spaces, to the extent that he consciously brings them together. This pattern is extended in a following episode when Tucker inadvertently brings an encroaching horde of reporters to his front door immediately after he is sacked, thus narrowing physically the gap between professional and private spaces. This notion is emphasised as, in the background of this exterior scene, a child's face is seen briefly at the window of Tucker's house, peering out at the massed crowds (see page 53). This glimpse of innocence reinforces the uncomfortable proximity of the two spheres at this point, further illustrating the extent to which characters can be made vulnerable in any location within this world.

We might relate the blurring of professional and domestic, public and private spaces in *The Thick of It* to a series of broadly acknowledged anxieties regarding 'work/life balance'. These concerns have become more acute in the twenty-first century due to the dramatic growth in mobile phone technology and electronic mail, advances that facilitate round-the-clock contact between work and home. In this sense, the physical boundaries between these two spheres have become increasingly less defined, rendering it more difficult for individuals to make the psychological distinction between their professional and domestic identities. This situation is exacerbated as emails and text messages, for example, are utilised for both work and leisure, and users employ social media like Facebook and Twitter to maintain their professional and personal profiles. It is clear that this kind of merging carries with it the potential for work pressures to invade domestic and leisure time, and it is partly for this reason that some workplaces – indeed, entire countries – seek to impose bans on email correspondence outside normal office hours. That kind of protection relies upon the basic assumption that there should be a difference between work and leisure time, or, more specifically, that the former should not be allowed to encroach upon the latter. *The Thick of It* resists this notion, however, as it consistently avoids showing any form of positive alternative to the relentless onslaught found in the corridors and offices of the political establishment. Dining rooms, factories, train carriages, hotels and kitchens offer no comfort or security for the individuals who inhabit them, and so the pressures of work are allowed to permeate these environments precisely because they do not disrupt or harm the overarching mood. In this way, a tonal relationship is established between all of the spaces in the programme as they each suppress and entrap characters. Taken together, these spaces combine to construct an entire fictional world that is bleak, unyielding and inhospitable. And so, with nowhere to hide, each character is caught in a continuing downward spiral, merely playing for time until that moment when they inevitably acquiesce to their world's merciless order.

5 Adaptation

The Thick of It has been adapted in two ways: the 2009 film *In the Loop* and the ongoing US television series *Veep* (2012–). It is worth emphasising an obvious point that neither of these represents a direct adaptation of the original television text. The decision not to 'remake' *The Thick of It* was perhaps influenced by an apparently disastrous attempt at making a straight US version of the programme for ABC in 2007. The resulting pilot did not persuade the network to pick up the show for its autumn schedule and Iannucci, one of its executive producers, has been scathing about the entire experience in interviews. The demise of the US version of *The Thick of It* is not unusual and the endeavour takes its place among a list of accomplished UK television comedies that failed to translate in similar ways, including *Dad's Army*, *Fawlty Towers*, *The Young Ones*, *Absolutely Fabulous*, *Men Behaving Badly*, *Cold Feet* and *Spaced*. The fortunes of UK television comedies adapted as films have been equally mixed and, whilst in recent years bland rehashes like *Are You Being Served?* (Bob Kellett, 1977) or *On the Buses* (Harry Booth, 1971) are less prevalent, it is still the case that successful programmes struggle to make the transition and releases such as *The Inbetweeners Movie* (Ben Palmer, 2011) or *Alan Partridge: Alpha Papa* (Declan Lowney, 2013) are balanced against *The League of Gentlemen's Apocalypse* (Steve Bendelack, 2005) or *Mrs Brown's Boys D'Movie* (Ben Kellett, 2014). *In the Loop* and *Veep* each sidestep some of these issues by functioning as significant departures from *The Thick of It*, adapting themes and ideas from the original programme but not replicating directly its dramatic settings. As a consequence, we might find ourselves more naturally inclined to view the film and the American television series as stand-alone achievements, rather than adjunct 'spin-offs'.

The Thick of It, *In the Loop* and *Veep* do share a core creative team, however. Iannucci is the consistent central element, having created all three productions and continuing as writer, director and producer on each, but *The Thick of It* writers Jesse Armstrong, Simon Blackwell, Tony Roche and Ian Martin also worked on *In the Loop*, and were joined by established colleagues Will Smith, Sean Gray, Roger Drew, Georgia Pritchett and David Quantick for the writing of *Veep*. In addition, *The Thick of It* cast member Chris Addison has directed episodes of the US show (and Peter Capaldi is likewise due to direct future episodes). This sharing of writing and production talent across the three titles provides not only a demonstration of Iannucci's capacity for collaboration but also secures a cohesive tone and style within the different projects. In addition, a number of cast members also play dual or multiple roles across *The Thick of It*, *In the Loop* and *Veep*. The existence of these discrete fictional worlds populated by the same faces with different names and backgrounds presents the notion that, although the situations and locations may shift and diverge, political hierarchies on both sides of the Atlantic contain certain character types that emerge in any given scenario. The reusing of actors makes a number of these characters interchangeable and, ironically, somewhat faceless: they are simply variant manifestations of each other. This point is illustrated in comedic fashion when Chris Addison's character in *In the Loop*, Toby, first enters the Department of International Development. As a new special adviser, he is greeted by the department's director of communications, Judy Molloy (Gina McKee), who wrongly identifies him as 'Dan'. Discovering her mistake, she apologises by saying: 'You guys are often called Dan, so it's worth a punt.' Addison, of course, plays special adviser Ollie Reeder in *The Thick of It*, and his depiction of Toby is almost identical, despite the fact that this is a different character in a new fictional setting. Judy's mistake with his name draws attention to the underlying lack of singular identity afforded to special advisers in these narratives – they could be called Ollie, Toby or even Dan and still possess near-identical traits, to the extent that specific names become only a minor consideration. This pattern is continued in the final moments of *In the Loop* when Toby is sacked and replaced by a character who is actually called Dan and is played by Will Smith, who also plays Ollie's rival special adviser Phil in *The Thick of It*.

The sharing of performers furthermore ensures that *The Thick of It*, *In the Loop* and *Veep* might be regarded as both continuous and discontinuous realities. They each represent potential versions of a world that we recognise and understand. The fact that some characters look and sound the same, but are different, conforms to the quantum relationship that is established between these texts: they exist simultaneously in divergent fictional realities. And, of course, the texts are potential versions of our world: mirrors of our reality. This fits with the allegorical nature of each production, attended to already in this book in relation to *The Thick of It*, whereby certain real-world facts and features are shared but are combined with imagined contexts and characters, and where direct reference to political parties and individuals is resisted. In this structure of parallel existences, the presence of Malcolm Tucker and Jamie McDonald as consistent characters in both *The Thick of It* and *In the Loop* is conceivably without issue, as it is possible that two quantum realities – in this case, fictional realities – would contain features that are exactly identical. We might reflect that it is simply poor fortune that two realities would share two characters who, in Tucker and Jamie, are defined by their aggressive amorality.

With these distinctions in mind, we can attend to the interests that *In the Loop* and *Veep* share, and which are held in common with *The Thick of It*. Given their status as political comedies, it is perhaps unsurprising to note that each text places the theme of power at its core. In approaching this subject, both *In the Loop* and *Veep* make the notion of powerlessness a central facet of their narratives, often depicting characters who are at the fringes of political influence and taking time to illustrate their impotence. *In the Loop* places Secretary of State for International Development, Simon Foster (Tom Hollander), within a struggle for power in the lead-up to an unspecified US-led war, a narrative that clearly echoes and critiques the events preceding the 2003 invasion of Iraq. Simon manages to embroil himself inadvertently in these manoeuvres through a series of ineloquent soundbites that variously endorse and challenge the case for war. As opposing factions within the US administration seize upon these pronouncements to strengthen their own competing causes, it becomes clear that Simon is being exploited for the limited value he holds within that political impasse and that, despite his claims of being a 'career politician' on the ascent, he actually exerts little real influence over events.

The stark contrast between Simon's professional existence and the upper echelons of US governance is exemplified when, having returned from Washington, he holds his local surgery in his constituency of the English town Northampton. At this surgery, an aggrieved local resident (played by Steve Coogan) complains to Simon about a constituency wall that is threatening to fall into his mother's garden. During the explanation of this issue, Simon receives a call from Karen Clark (Mimi Kennedy), US Assistant Secretary of State for Diplomacy, patched through from London. Simon elects to take the call in an adjoining side room away from the now irate resident, although the man's shouting can still be heard in the background. Indeed, Karen comments on the noise and, when she asks Simon about it, he explains that it is 'departmental business. It's about a wall.' Without missing a beat, Karen asks 'Gaza?', to which Simon responds with a weak affirmative. There is an obvious gulf between Karen's assumption that Simon is referring to a landmark of international conflict and the reality that he is in fact dealing with a small boundary wall that threatens to damage an elderly lady's greenhouse. The contrast between Washington and Northampton is further exemplified as Simon stands in the dreary surroundings of a church hall, replete with stacked plastic chairs and safety notices, while Karen is seated at her desk in her opulent, warmly lit, glass-walled office (see page 54). It makes sense, then, that Karen should be calling Simon to admonish him for not supporting her properly when he visited Washington, emphasising her status as his superior despite his later protestations that she is not his boss (which he makes after the call has ended, rather than directly to Karen). This exchange fits with a pattern in the film of Simon's sense of his own power and influence on the international stage being undermined and it is apt that, when he belatedly decides to take a stand against the war, he is sacked ostensibly because that precarious constituency wall has fallen into the neighbour's garden. We are therefore entitled to note that *In the Loop* makes an effective power distinction between US and UK political systems. And yet, even characters on the US side are subject to equivalent curtailments. Karen Clark, for example, ends the film having failed to stop the war and is no longer in office, as she resigns from her post – a gesture that loses its dramatic impact when a key colleague, General Miller (James Gandolfini), reneges on a pact they had made earlier and declines to submit his own resignation letter. As her endeavours have almost no lasting impact on the direction of events, Karen is united with Simon when their final acts of political decisiveness become futile, self-defeating gestures.

This theme of impotency is picked up and intensified in *Veep*. For the first three seasons of the show, Vice-President Selina Meyer (Julia Louis-Dreyfus) finds her professional influence stunted by the inherent limitations of her role. Although she is trapped in this status quo, we are certainly encouraged to form the enduring impression that Selina is in any case ill-equipped for positions of responsibility, as her competency falls some way behind her careerist ambitions. As a brief early illustration of this, in the second episode of series one, Selina is temporarily required to fulfil the role of president as the present incumbent has been taken ill with chest pains. The process of relaying this information to Selina is delayed, as she is in the middle of berating the 'shit-for-brains president' to the member of his staff (Jonah Ryan, played by Timothy Simons) charged with delivering the news to her. On arriving at the president's offices, a secretary briefs

Selina and, during this speech, the vice-president is visibly unfocused and disconcerted, looking very much like a small child in an adult's world and consequently displaying her lack of proficiency in the role. Her first act in temporary office is to deliver an ineloquent homage to the current president and then, while her personal aide, Gary Walsh (Tony Hale), vomits audibly in the background due to a virus he has recently contracted, she asks those assembled in the room to join her in a short, incoherent, prayer. Both events are self-indulgent, awkward and out of step with the tone and mood of the professional environment in which they take place. Selina's stint as temporary president is cut short, however, as minutes later she is informed that she can stand down, as the incumbent president was only experiencing heartburn rather than a serious medical condition. Barely managing to mask her stabbing disappointment behind a rigid smile, Selina departs the briefing room. She belatedly remembers to give back the documents and the pen she had been using, inadvertently emphasising the fact that she was only ever visiting the seat of office. After leaving, unseen by anyone else, Selina pokes her head back around the door, as though savouring a last glimpse of the room in which she almost wielded actual power.

Veep (2012–)

Instances of this kind are typical of *Veep*, as Selina is always at the periphery of events and, as a consequence, is able only to react to them with varying degrees of competency. As it centres upon Selina, the world of *Veep* is rendered chaotic and shambolic, lacking the smooth character-led structure and purpose of White House-based US shows such as *House of Cards* and *The West Wing* (1999–2006). Indeed, *Veep* rejects the notion of a political survival based on the formulation and enacting of careful plans, and instead creates scenarios in which Selina and her team repeatedly mishandle situations, to the extent that their successes are defined almost exclusively by their ability to mask their errors.

Given the peripheral role afforded the vice-president in *Veep*, we might be inclined to suggest that the incompetence of Selina and her staff has limited consequence: that the programme creates a 'safe' environment in which characters are permitted their comically appalling behaviour. And yet, that brief scene in which Selina is asked to temporarily become president also provides a reminder of her potential proximity to real power. Indeed, when she enters the room, she is briefed on a number of serious matters that will require her attention. Her bewilderment not only conveys how unsuited she is for such duties but also emphasises the danger of such a person being placed anywhere near this role. This small motif is played out again on a larger scale when, at the end of the third season, Selina actually becomes president and, if anything, her lack of competence in office becomes more pronounced as she experiences this new pressure. In its depiction and handling of Selina's character, *Veep* offers a relentless critique of a political system in which authority can be handed to individuals who lack the necessary credentials to wield that power carefully, thoughtfully and responsibly. As a result, the programme provides not only a satire of US politics but also a stark reminder of the need for accountability and transparency in that system. Selina's success is measured almost entirely by the media responses to her actions, a theme that carries over from *The Thick of It*, and the programme penetrates that central issue of discrepancy between public perceptions of political figures and their actual behaviours. Rather than allowing audiences to dismiss politics entirely because it is populated by idiots and miscreants, *Veep* might encourage us to engage with politics more carefully, to pay closer attention precisely because those seeking election to office may be unfit to govern.

Veep's contention that access to power has the potential to be dangerous, especially when it is placed in the wrong hands, can be related back to *In the Loop*. Making clear reference to the events leading up to the invasion of Iraq, the film provides a more direct and vehement critique of political processes than perhaps either *The Thick of It* or *Veep* attempt. Here, events are not held at the periphery occupied by characters like Simon Foster and power is not handed only to fools. Instead, unscrupulous individuals working away from the public gaze hold profound influence. In one breathless and pivotal sequence, Malcolm Tucker and Jamie McDonald set about rewriting a report so that it no longer provides an uncommitted stance upon military action but rather an unequivocal endorsement of it. We cut between Tucker and Toby crouched over a stack of papers and a laptop in the UN building in Washington and Jamie with a Foreign Office director, Michael Rodgers (James Smith), positioned in front of a laptop at Westminster. Whilst on the phone to Tucker, Jamie is forcing Michael to delete and revise entire sections of the report. At one point, Tucker instructs that they delete numerous pages of caveats that advise against military action and Michael hesitates, protesting quietly that 'You can't delete the arguments against the war.' Jamie reports Michael's reluctance and Tucker suggests that he gives him a thump; instead, Jamie takes Michael's finger and forcibly makes him delete the sections, thus completing the task. The crude physical invasiveness of this gesture, coupled with Michael's pained resignation as it takes place, emphasises the atrocious violation that is enacted. The simple click of the key as the sections are deleted lends a brutal simplicity to an action that will result in pain and death for thousands of people when the war, which Tucker and Jamie are seeking to contrive, fully begins.

Whether acting upon their misguided careerist ambitions or out of a desire to manipulate the truth for political gain, characters in *Veep* and *In the Loop* consistently display a disregard for the responsibility that accompanies power: they simply crave that power. Indeed, it is not difficult to characterise their attitudes as inherently cynical, continuing a pattern established by character behaviours in *The Thick of It*. We might be tempted to extend this notion by concluding that each text is equally cynical about the political environment it seeks to depict and, furthermore, that *The Thick of It*, *In the Loop* and *Veep* are cynical about politics in general. This may be where political commentator Michael White's discomfort with *The Thick of It* stems from, as he perceives that it 'lacked heart, lacked sympathy, lacked good guys, let alone honest ambition' (White, 2009). And, as the central creative force behind each of these productions, it is perhaps tempting to associate these attitudes with Iannucci himself. This is certainly the position taken by Steven Fielding when, commenting upon Iannucci's call for people to exercise their voting rights during the 2015 British election campaign, he suggests that:

> it is rather paradoxical for Iannucci to now suggest Britons should vote for those politicians he has spent his career ridiculing. This is especially the case when he has arguably made a significant contribution to the very apathy against which he rails. In an age of mass ignorance about how parliamentary politics actually works, comedies like The Thick of It are one of the few means by which millions of Britons now get their information about how they are governed – and there are any number of audience surveys that show that what an audience sees on the screen about politics, they tend to believe. (Fielding, 2015)

We might reflect that, if *The Thick of It* really is 'one of the few means by which millions of Britons now get their information about how they are governed', there is a greater issue regarding the whole process of political communication and how it has become so impoverished. Leaving those concerns aside, Fielding's position represents a way of interpreting Iannucci's creative work that supposes his authorial intentions to be as negative as the attitudes of those held by the characters on screen. It is equally possible (if not probable, given Iannucci's public endorsement of democratic action, which Fielding mentions) that *The Thick of It*, *In the Loop* and *Veep* might counter voter apathy precisely by illustrating the consequences of inept, unscrupulous or – indeed – apathetic individuals holding positions of governance. In this respect, Iannucci's works approach the subject of political power with exceptional seriousness, laying out the consequent dangers that a public lack of involvement with the political process can court. One of Iannucci's achievements is to make such statements engaging and funny, but it is never the case that comedic form necessarily negates sincerity. It seems more appropriate, then, to conclude that *The Thick of It*, *In the Loop* and *Veep* promote awareness and vigilance as necessary virtues, rather than inviting apathy. Such concerns range more broadly than the immediate political context and can be read as enduring warnings about the ways in which power can be wielded undemocratically or unethically. The abuse of power is not the sole preserve of the political establishment and we are surely not meant to regard Iannucci's texts as only direct responses to very particular political contexts. That is certainly not the experience one gains from watching Selina Meyer or Malcolm Tucker come alive on screen. These characters move beyond the real-world equivalents who may have inspired their creation, becoming fictional realities in their own right. As these characters transcend notions of linear political commentary, the implicit point is made that individuals of this kind might be found anywhere. Egotists and bullies exist in every professional environment on earth. Perhaps you've met some. And perhaps we should not be surprised by the fact that we recognise the behaviour of our elected leaders in comedic storylines about second-home scandals, illegal wars or unregulated lobbying and, instead, consider why we are able to make such connections so readily. We might ask what those easy associations tell us about the standard of political representation in the UK and US, past, present and future.

Notes

1 It would be wrong, however, to suggest that a natural correspondence exists between a programme's popularity with viewers and the critical or scholarly attention it receives. Brett Mills, for example, defines 'invisible television' as programmes which 'despite long running and consistently garnering high audience ratings, are repeatedly ignored by the vast majority of academic work' (Mills, 2010, p. 1).

2 Iannucci and Morris also wrote *The Day Today*, along with Peter Baynham and a cast including Steve Coogan, David Schneider and Rebecca Front. A further team of writers, including Graham Linehan and Arthur Mathews, provided additional material.

3 The US version of *House of Cards* replaces the departing Thatcher imagery with the central character, now Frank Underwood rather than Urquhart, putting a fatally injured dog out of its misery by strangulation. A more direct introduction, certainly, but one that perhaps conjures a series of rather unfortunate analogies.

Bibliography

BBC Trust, 'BBC Two Service Licence', April 2014a. Available at: <http://www.bbc.co.uk/bbctrust/our_work/services/television/service_licences/bbc_two.html>. Accessed 6 January 2016.

BBC Trust, 'BBC Four Service Licence', April 2014b. Available at: <http://www.bbc.co.uk/bbctrust/our_work/services/television/service_licences/bbc_four.html>. Accessed 6 January 2016.

Brown, Tom, *Breaking the Fourth Wall: Direct Address in the Cinema* (Edinburgh: Edinburgh University Press, 2013).

Campbell, Alastair, *The Alastair Campbell Diaries Volume 1: Prelude to Power 1994–1997* (London: Random House, 2010).

———, *The Alastair Campbell Diaries Volume 3: Power & Responsibility 1999–2001* (London: Random House, 2011).

Editorial, 'The Thick of It: Long Live Tucker', *Observer*, 28 October 2012.

Fielding, Steve, 'Armando Iannucci Is a Hypocrite for Demanding Britons Vote', *The Conversation*, 17 February 2015. Available at: <http://theconversation.com/armando-ianucci-is-a-hypocrite-for-demanding-britons-vote-37665>. Accessed 6 January 2016.

Fiske, John and John Hartley, *Reading Television* (London: Methuen, 1978).

Gray, Sean, 'The Thick of It: When Life Imitates Sweary Art', *BBC Magazine*, 13 October 2012.

Iannucci, Armando, 'Yes, Minister: Nothing Changes', *Daily Telegraph*, 7 February 2004.

Jones, Nicholas, *Sultans of Spin: The Media and the New Labour Government* (London: Orion, 1999).

Kilborn, Richard, *Staging the Real: Factual TV Programming in the Age of 'Big Brother'* (Manchester: Manchester University Press, 2003).

Lury, Karen, *Interpreting Television* (London: Hodder, 2005).

McBride, Damian, *Power Trip: A Decade of Policy, Plots and Spin* (London: Biteback, 2013).

McPherson, Fiona, 'The Oxford Dictionaries UK Word of the Year 2012 Is "Omnishambles"', *Oxford Dictionaries*, 12 November 2012.

Mills, Brett, 'Invisible Television: The Programmes No One Talks about Even Though Lots of People Watch Them', *Critical Studies in Television* vol. 5 no. 1 (Spring 2010), pp. 1–16.

Moore, Martin, *The Origins of Modern Spin: Democratic Government and the Media in Britain, 1945–51* (London: Palgrave Macmillan, 2006).

Mulvey, Laura, *Citizen Kane* (London: BFI, 1992).

Neather, Andrew, 'Chloe Smithwatch; the Hapless Minister Is Back on TV', *Evening Standard*, 23 August 2012.

O'Carroll, Lisa, 'Andy Coulson Jailed for 18 Months for Conspiracy to Hack Phones', *Guardian*, 4 July 2014.

O'Neill, Brendan, 'Blair's Dodgy Dossier', *Spiked*, 24 September 2002. Available at: <http://www.spiked-online.com/newsite/article/4905#.Voz745OLRxg>. Accessed 6 January 2016.

Owen, Paul, 'Business Bank: Has Vince Cable Been Watching The Thick of It?', *Guardian*, 24 September 2012.

Perkins, V. F., *Film as Film: Understanding and Judging Movies* (New York: Da Capo Press, 1993).

Public Administration Select Committee, 'Special Advisers in the Thick of It', *House of Commons*, 14 October 2012.

Richards, Paul, *Be Your Own Spin Doctor: A Practical Guide to Using the Media* (Manchester: Take That, 1998).

Smith, Murray, *Engaging Characters: Fiction, Emotion and the Cinema* (Oxford: Oxford University Press, 1995).

Thomas, Deborah, *Reading Hollywood: Spaces and Meanings in American Film* (London: Wallflower, 2001).

Walters, Ben, *The Office* (London: BFI, 2005).

Wardrop, Murray, 'Peter Capaldi: Thick of It Spin Doctor Malcolm Tucker Was Not Based on Alastair Campbell', *Daily Telegraph*, 31 January 2012.

White, Michael, 'The Thick of It: Cynical, Cruel and Lacking in Heart', *Guardian*, 23 October 2009.

Wintour, Patrick, 'Labour Fury as David Cameron Tells Angela Eagle: "Calm Down, Dear"', *Guardian*, 27 April 2011.

Wollaston, Sam, 'The Thick of It and Casualty', *Guardian*, 26 October 2009.

Wood, Robin, *Hitchcock's Films* (London: A. Zwemmer, 1965).

Zborowski, James, 'The Presentation of Detail and the Organisation of Time in *The Royle Family*', in Jason Jacobs and Steven Peacock (eds), *Television Aesthetics and Style* (London: Bloomsbury, 2013).

bfi tv classics

Credits

The Thick of It

United Kingdom/2005 &
2009–12
United Kingdom/United
States/2007

four series, three specials

series 1, episode 1
(1st tx Thursday, 19 May
2005, BBC Four; 22:30–
23:00) (29m 18s)

directed and devised by
Armando Iannucci
producer
Adam Tandy
written by
Jesse Armstrong
Armando Iannucci
additional material
the Cast
Sam Bain
Ian Martin
director of photography
Jamie Cairney
editor
Billy Sneddon
production designer
Simon Rogers

©2005 BBC
Production Company
BBC

executive producer
Jon Plowman
production executive
Jez Nightingale
production manager
Francis Gilson
production coordinator
Natalie Bailey
location manager
Tom Howard
production runner
Simon Judd

production accountant
Kelley James
post-production
Framestore CFC
2nd assistant director
Natalie Segal
script supervisor
Suzanne Baron
casting director
Sarah Crowe
script consultant
Martin Sixsmith
camera operator
Ben Wheeler
gaffer
Colin Thwaites
art director
Martina O'Loughlin
props master
David Oakham
standby props
Derek O'Brian
production buyer
Laura Marsh
costume designer
Ros Little
wardrobe supervisor
Janine Marr
make-up designer
Judith Barkas
make-up assistant
Jayne Buxton
sound recordist
Chris Round
boom operator
Luke Neumann
dubbing editor
Chris Maclean

cast
Chris Langham
Hugh Abbot
Peter Capaldi
Malcolm Tucker
Chris Addison
Oliver Reeder
Joanna Scanlan
Terri Coverley

James Smith
Glenn Cullen
Timothy Bentinck
Cliff Lawton
John Biggins
driver
Lucinda Raikes
Angela Heaney

series 1, episode 2
(1st tx Thursday, 26 May
2005, BBC Four; 22:30–
23:00) (29m 7s)

directed and devised by
Armando Iannucci
producer
Adam Tandy
written by
Simon Blackwell
Tony Roche
additional material
the Cast
Ian Martin
director of photography
Jamie Cairney
editor
Billy Sneddon
production designer
Simon Rogers

©2005 BBC
Production Company
BBC

executive producer
Jon Plowman
production executive
Jez Nightingale
production manager
Francis Gilson
production coordinator
Natalie Bailey
location manager
Tom Howard
production runner
Simon Judd

the thick of it

production accountant
Kelley James
post-production
Framestore CFC
2nd assistant director
Natalie Segal
script supervisor
Suzanne Baron
casting director
Sarah Crowe
script consultant
Martin Sixsmith
camera operator
Ben Wheeler
gaffer
Colin Thwaites
art director
Martina O'Loughlin
props master
David Oakham
standby props
Derek O'Brian
production buyer
Laura Marsh
costume designer
Ros Little
wardrobe supervisor
Janine Marr
make-up designer
Judith Barkas
make-up assistant
Jayne Buxton
sound recordist
Chris Round
boom operator
Luke Neumann
dubbing editor
Chris Maclean

cast
Chris Langham
Hugh Abbot
Peter Capaldi
Malcolm Tucker
Chris Addison
Oliver Reeder
Joanna Scanlan
Terri Coverley
James Smith
Glenn Cullen
Morwenna Banks
Mary
Matthew Marsh
Simon Hewitt

series 1, episode 3
(1st tx Thursday, 2 June 2005,
BBC Four; 22:30–23:00)
(29m 12s)

directed and devised by
Armando Iannucci
producer
Adam Tandy
written by
Jesse Armstrong
Simon Blackwell
Armando Iannucci
additional material
the Cast
Ian Martin
director of photography
Jamie Cairney
editor
Billy Sneddon
production designer
Simon Rogers

©2005 BBC
Production Company
BBC

executive producer
Jon Plowman
production executive
Jez Nightingale
production manager
Francis Gilson
production coordinator
Natalie Bailey
location manager
Tom Howard
production runner
Simon Judd
production accountant
Kelley James
post-production
Framestore CFC
2nd assistant director
Natalie Segal
script supervisor
Suzanne Baron
casting director
Sarah Crowe
script consultant
Martin Sixsmith
camera operator
Ben Wheeler
gaffer
Colin Thwaites

art director
Martina O'Loughlin
props master
David Oakham
standby props
Derek O'Brian
production buyer
Laura Marsh
costume designer
Ros Little
wardrobe supervisor
Janine Marr
make-up designer
Judith Barkas
make-up assistant
Jayne Buxton
sound recordist
Chris Round
boom operator
Luke Neumann
dubbing editor
Chris Maclean

cast
Chris Langham
Hugh Abbot
Peter Capaldi
Malcolm Tucker
Chris Addison
Oliver Reeder
Joanna Scanlan
Terri Coverley
James Smith
Glenn Cullen
Tony Gardner
Dan Miller
Georgie Glen
Susan Dorling
Lucinda Raikes
Angela Heaney

series 2, episode 1
(1st tx Thursday, 20 October
2005, BBC Four;
22:30–23:00) (29m 21s)

directed and devised by
Armando Iannucci
producer
Adam Tandy
written by
Jesse Armstrong
with
Simon Blackwell
Armando Iannucci

bfi tv classics

Tony Roche
additional material
Ian Martin
the Cast
director of photography
Jamie Cairney
editor
David Frisby
production designer
Simon Rogers

©2005 BBC
Production Company
BBC

executive producer
Jon Plowman
production executive
Jez Nightingale
production manager
Gayle Cope
production coordinator
Lucy Crayford
location manager
Chris May
production runner
Harriet Bowden
production accountant
Robin Hester
post-production
Evolutions
1st assistant director
Cordelia Hardy
2nd assistant director
Jonny Benson
script supervisor
Julie Church-Benns
casting director
Sarah Crowe
script consultant
Martin Sixsmith
camera operator
Greg Duffield
gaffer
Darren Jackson
art director
Martina O'Loughlin
props master
David Oakham
standby props
Derek O'Brian
production buyer
Laura Marsh
costume designer
Jackie Vernon

wardrobe supervisor
Janine Marr
make-up designer
Judith Barkas
make-up supervisor
Jayne Buxton
sound recordists
Bob Newton
Andrey Halley
boom [operator]
Richard Pilcher
dubbing editor
Chris Maclean
with thanks to
BBC America

cast
Chris Langham
Hugh Abbot
Peter Capaldi
Malcolm Tucker
Chris Addison
Oliver Reeder
James Smith
Glenn Cullen
Polly Kemp
Robyn Murdoch
Di Botcher
Pauline McKendrick
Robert Portal
Mark Davies
Graeme Mearns
Frankie
Paul Higgins
Jamie
Rob Edwards
Geoff Holhurst
Theo Fraser Steele
Christian Holhurst

series 2, episode 2
(1st tx Thursday, 27 October 2005, BBC Four; 22:30–23:00) (29m 19s)

directed and devised by
Armando Iannucci
producer
Adam Tandy
written by
Jesse Armstrong
Simon Blackwell
Armando Iannucci
Tony Roche

additional material
Ian Martin
the Cast
director of photography
Jamie Cairney
editor
David Frisby
production designer
Simon Rogers

©2005 BBC
Production Company
BBC

executive producer
Jon Plowman
production executive
Jez Nightingale
production manager
Gayle Cope
production coordinator
Lucy Crayford
location manager
Chris May
production runner
Harriet Bowden
production accountant
Robin Hester
post-production
Evolutions
1st assistant director
Cordelia Hardy
2nd assistant director
Jonny Benson
script supervisor
Julie Church-Benns
casting director
Sarah Crowe
script consultant
Martin Sixsmith
camera operator
Greg Duffield
gaffer
Darren Jackson
art director
Martina O'Loughlin
props master
David Oakham
standby props
Derek O'Brian
production buyer
Laura Marsh

the thick of it

costume designer
Jackie Vernon
wardrobe supervisor
Janine Marr
make-up supervisor
Jayne Buxton
make-up assistant
Cathy Burczak
sound recordist
Bob Newton
boom [operator]
Richard Pilcher
dubbing editor
Chris Maclean
with thanks to
BBC America

cast
Chris Langham
Hugh Abbot
Peter Capaldi
Malcolm Tucker
Chris Addison
Oliver Reeder
James Smith
Glenn Cullen
Polly Kemp
Robyn Murdoch
Joanna Scanlan
Terri Coverley
Alex Macqueen
Julius Nicholson
Lucinda Raikes
Angela Heaney
James Doherty
Steve
Graeme Mearns
Frankie
Richard Betts
online *Telegraph*

series 2, episode 3
(1st tx Thursday, 3 November 2005, BBC Four;
22:30–23:00) (29m 17s)

directed and devised by
Armando Iannucci
producer
Adam Tandy
written by
Simon Blackwell
Tony Roche
with
Jesse Armstrong
Armando Iannucci

additional material
Ian Martin
the Cast
director of photography
Jamie Cairney
editor
David Frisby
production designer
Simon Rogers

©2005 BBC
Production Company
BBC

executive producer
Jon Plowman
production executive
Jez Nightingale
production managers
Alison Passey
Gayle Cope
production coordinator
Lucy Crawford [Crayford]
location manager
Chris May
production runner
Harriet Bowden
production accountant
Robin Hester
post-production
Evolutions
1st assistant director
Cordelia Hardy
2nd assistant director
Jonny Benson
script supervisor
Julie Church-Benns
casting director
Sarah Crowe
script consultant
Martin Sixsmith
camera operators
Ben Wheeler
Greg Duffield
gaffer
Colin Thwaites
art director
Martina O'Loughlin
props master
David Oakham
standby props
Derek O'Brian
production buyer
Laura Marsh

costume designer
Ros Little
wardrobe supervisor
Janine Marr
make-up supervisor
Jayne Buxton
make-up assistant
Cathy Burczak
sound recordist
Bob Newton
boom [operator]
Richard Pilcher
dubbing editor
Chris Maclean
with thanks to
BBC America

cast
Chris Langham
Hugh Abbot
Peter Capaldi
Malcolm Tucker
Chris Addison
Oliver Reeder
Joanna Scanlan
Terri Coverley
James Smith
Glenn Cullen
Polly Kemp
Robyn Murdoch
Eve Matheson
Claire Ballantine
Martin Ball
Roy Smedley

special #1

Rise of the Nutters [billing title only]
(1st tx Sunday, 1 July 2007, BBC Four; 21:00–22:00)
(59m 12s)

directed and devised by
Armando Iannucci
producer
Adam Tandy
series producer
Armando Iannucci
written by
Jesse Armstrong
Simon Blackwell
Armando Iannucci
Tony Roche
additional material
Ian Martin

bfi tv classics

the Cast
director of photography
Ben Wheeler
editors
Ant Boys
Billy Sneddon
production designer
Simon Rogers

©2007 BBC
Production Companies
BBC/BBC America
co-production

executive producer
Jon Plowman
production executive
Jez Nightingale
production manager
Grace Boylan
assistant producer
Natalie Bailey
production coordinator
Sarah Benneworth
location manager
Simon Scott
unit manager
Ali Bryer Carron
runner
Nick Dennis
team assistant
Sean Gray
production accountant
Harjeet Ghataora
post-production
Framestore CFC
1st assistant director
Chris May
2nd assistant director
Lisa Thornton
script supervisor
Suzanne Baron
casting director
Sarah Crowe
B camera operator
Greg Duffield
gaffer
Colin Thwaites
art director
Mel Stenhouse
props master
Dave Oakham
standby props
Michala Jermy

production buyer
Laurie Law
costume designer
Jackie Vernon
wardrobe supervisor
Anita Lad
make-up designer
Judith Barkas
make-up artist
Nuala McArdle
sound recordist
Bob Newton
boom [operator]
Richard Pilcher
dubbing mixer
Chris Maclean
dubbing editor
Will Cohen

cast
Peter Capaldi
Malcolm Tucker
Chris Addison
Oliver Reeder
Joanna Scanlan
Terri Coverley
James Smith
Glenn Cullen
Justin Edwards
Ben Swain
Paul Higgins
Jamie
Alex Macqueen
Julius Nicholson
Roger Allam
Peter Mannion
Vincent Franklin
Stewart Pearson
Olivia Poulet
Emma Messinger
Will Smith
Phil Smith
Lucinda Raikes
Angela Heaney
David Dawson
Affers

special #2

Spinners and Losers [billing title only]
(1st tx Tuesday, 3 July 2007, BBC Four; 21.00–22.00)
(58m 59s)

directed and devised by
Armando Iannucci
producer
Adam Tandy
series producer
Armando Iannucci
written by
Jesse Armstrong
Simon Blackwell
Armando Iannucci
Tony Roche
additional material
Ian Martin
the Cast
director of photography
Jamie Cairney
editors
Ant Boys
Billy Sneddon
production designer
Simon Rogers

©2007 BBC
Production Companies
BBC/BBC America
co-production

executive producer
Jon Plowman
production executive
Jez Nightingale
production manager
Grace Boylan
assistant producer
Natalie Bailey
production coordinator
Nila Karadia
unit manager
Ali Bryer Carron
location manager
Simon Scott
production runners
Simon Cooper
Nicholas Searle
production accountant
Klaudia Mejcz
post-production
Framestore CFC
1st assistant director
Chris May
2nd assistant director
Lisa Thornton
script supervisor
Wendy Poon

the thick of it

casting director
Sarah Crowe
script consultants
Martin Sixsmith
Kate Conway
B camera operator
Ben Wheeler
gaffer
Colin Thwaites
art director
Thorin Thompson
props master
Dave Oakham
standby props
Sam Harley
production buyer
Laurie Law
costume designer
Jackie Vernon
wardrobe supervisor
Anita Lad
make-up designer
Jayne Buxton
make-up artist
Cathy Burczak
sound recordist
Bob Newton
boom [operator]
Richard Pilcher
dubbing editor
Chris Maclean

cast
Peter Capaldi
Malcolm Tucker
Chris Addison
Oliver Reeder
James Smith
Glenn Cullen
Joanna Scanlan
Terri Coverley
Polly Kemp
Robyn Murdoch
Lucinda Raikes
Angela Heaney
Tony Gardner
Dan Miller
Ben Willbond
Adam Kenyon
Timothy Bentinck
Cliff Lawton
Rob Edwards
Geoff Holhurst
Martin Savage
Nick Hanway

Paul Higgins
Jamie
Justin Edwards
Ben Swain
Alex Macqueen
Julius Nicholson
Eve Matheson
Clare Ballentine
Diveen Henry
Elizabeth

special #3

**The Thick of It Special
Spinners and Losers New,
extended edition [billing title]
aka Opposition Extra**
(1st tx Wednesday, 10 October
2007, BBC Four; 00.00–
00.15) (14m 48s)

directed and devised by
Armando Iannucci
producer
Adam Tandy
series producer
Armando Iannucci
written by
Jesse Armstrong
Simon Blackwell
Armando Iannucci
Tony Roche
additional material
Ian Martin
the Cast
director of photography
Jamie Cairney
editors
Ant Boys
Billy Sneddon
production designer
Simon Rogers

©2007 BBC
Production Companies
BBC/BBC America
co-production

executive producer
Jon Plowman
production executive
Jez Nightingale
production manager
Grace Boylan

assistant producer
Natalie Bailey
production coordinator
Nila Karadia
unit manager
Ali Bryer Carron
location manager
Simon Scott
production runners
Simon Cooper
Nicholas Searle
production accountant
Klaudia Mejcz
post-production
Framestore CFC
1st assistant director
Chris May
2nd assistant director
Lisa Thornton
script supervisor
Wendy Poon
casting director
Sarah Crowe
script consultants
Martin Sixsmith
Kate Conway
B camera operator
Ben Wheeler
gaffer
Colin Thwaites
art director
Thorin Thompson
props master
Dave Oakham
standby props
Sam Harley
production buyer
Laurie Law
costume designer
Jackie Vernon
wardrobe supervisor
Anita Lad
make-up designer
Jayne Buxton
make-up artist
Cathy Burczak
sound recordist
Bob Newton
boom [operator]
Richard Pilcher
dubbing editor
Chris Maclean

cast
Roger Allam
Peter Mannion

bfi tv classics

Vincent Franklin
Stewart Pearson
Olivia Poulet
Emma Messinger
Will Smith
Phil Smith
Ben Willbond
Adam Kenyon
Lucinda Raikes
Angela Heaney
Chris Addison
Oliver Reeder
David Dawson
Affers
Justin Edwards
Ben Swain

series 3, episode 1
(1st tx Saturday, 24 October 2009, BBC Two; 22:10–22:40) (30m 0s)

directed and devised by
Armando Iannucci
produced by
Adam Tandy
written by
Simon Blackwell
with
Jesse Armstrong
Roger Drew
and
Will Smith
Sean Gray
Armando Iannucci
Ian Martin
Tony Roche
additional material
the Cast
director of photography
Jamie Cairney
editor
Ant Boys
production designer
Simon Rogers

©2009 BBC
Production Company
BBC

executive producers
Mark Freeland
Armando Iannucci
production executive
Sarah Hitchcock

production manager
Catherine Gosling
production coordinator
Lauriel Martin
location manager
Tom Howard
unit manager
Patrick Burrows
production runner
Louis Maunder
production accountant
Owain Jonkers
post-production
Framestore
1st assistant director
Charlie Leech
2nd assistant director
Jon Jennings
3rd assistant director
Daniel Castella
director's assistant
Will Smith
script supervisor
Elise Burgess
casting director
Sarah Crowe
script consultants
Martin Sixsmith
Kate Conway
research
Jackie Ramsamy
B camera operator
Greg Duffield
camera assistants
Gary Rogers
Tom Vincent
gaffer
Colin Thwaites
art director
Holly Berk
props master
Craig Price
standby props
Paul Mitchell
production buyer
Laura Marsh
props storeman
Laurence Archer
graphic artist
Barry Sexton
costume designer
Ros Little
costume supervisor
Janine Marr
make-up designer

Judith Barkas
make-up artist
Nuala McArdle
sound recordist
Bob Newton
boom [operator]
Richard Pilcher
dubbing editor
Chris Maclean

cast
Peter Capaldi
Malcolm Tucker
Rebecca Front
Nicola Murray
Chris Addison
Oliver Reeder
Joanna Scanlan
Terri Coverley
James Smith
Glenn Cullen
Pearce Quigley
Doug Hayes
Rory Kinnear
Ed

series 3, episode 2
(1st tx Saturday, 31 October 2009 on BBC Two; 22:10–22:40) (29m 15s)

directed and devised by
Armando Iannucci
produced by
Adam Tandy
written by
Jesse Armstrong
with
Simon Blackwell
Roger Drew
and
Will Smith
Sean Gray
Armando Iannucci
Ian Martin
Tony Roche
additional material
the Cast
director of photography
Jamie Cairney
editor
Ant Boys
production designer
Simon Rogers

the thick of it

©2009 BBC
Production Company
BBC
executive producers
Mark Freeland
Armando Iannucci
production executive
Sarah Hitchcock
production manager
Catherine Gosling
production coordinator
Lauriel Martin
location manager
Tom Howard
unit manager
Patrick Burrows
production runner
Louis Maunder
production accountant
Owain Jonkers
post-production
Framestore
1st assistant director
Charlie Leech
2nd assistant director
Jon Jennings
3rd assistant director
Daniel Castella
director's assistant
Will Smith
script supervisor
Elise Burgess
casting director
Sarah Crowe
script consultants
Martin Sixsmith
Kate Conway
B camera operator
Greg Duffield
gaffer
Colin Thwaites
best boy
Richard Potter
art director
Holly Berk
props master
Craig Price
standby props
Paul Mitchell
production buyer
Laura Marsh
graphic artist
Barry Sexton

costume designer
Ros Little
costume supervisor
Janine Marr
costume assistant
Eleanor Spalding
make-up designer
Judith Barkas
make-up artist
Nuala McArdle
make-up assistant
Katy Richards
sound recordist
Bob Newton
boom [operator]
Richard Pilcher
B boom
Ben Coleman
dubbing editor
Chris Maclean

cast
Peter Capaldi
Malcolm Tucker
Rebecca Front
Nicola Murray
Chris Addison
Oliver Reeder
Joanna Scanlan
Terri Coverley
James Smith
Glenn Cullen
Polly Kemp
Robyn Murdoch
Peter Sullivan
Geoffrey
Alex Lowe
John
Judith Faultless
journalist
Zoë Telford
Marianne Swift

series 3, episode 3
(1st tx Saturday, 7 November 2009 on BBC Two;
22:15–22:45) (29m 19s)

directed and devised by
Armando Iannucci
produced by
Adam Tandy
written by
Tony Roche

with
Jesse Armstrong
Simon Blackwell
Roger Drew
and
Will Smith
Sean Gray
Armando Iannucci
Ian Martin
additional material
the Cast
director of photography
Jamie Cairney
editor
Gary Dollner
production designer
Simon Rogers

©2009 BBC
Production Company
BBC

executive producers
Mark Freeland
Armando Iannucci
production executive
Sarah Hitchcock
production manager
Catherine Gosling
production coordinator
Lauriel Martin
location manager
Tom Howard
unit manager
Patrick Burrows
production runner
Louis Maunder
production accountant
Owain Jonkers
post-production
Framestore
1st assistant director
Charlie Leech
2nd assistant director
Jon Jennings
3rd assistant director
Daniel Castella
director's assistant
Will Smith
script supervisor
Elise Burgess
casting director
Sarah Crowe
script consultants
Martin Sixsmith

bfi tv classics

Kate Conway
B camera operator
Greg Duffield
camera assistants
Gary Rogers
Tom Vincent
gaffer
Colin Thwaites
best boy
Richard Potter
art director
Holly Berk
props master
Craig Price
standby props
Paul Mitchell
production buyer
Laura Marsh
props storeman
Laurence Archer
costume designer
Ros Little
costume supervisor
Janine Marr
costume assistant
Eleanor Spalding
make-up designer
Judith Barkas
make-up artist
Nuala McArdle
make-up assistant
Katy Richards
sound recordist
Bob Newton
boom [operator]
Richard Pilcher
B boom
Ben Coleman
dubbing editor
Chris Maclean

cast
Peter Capaldi
Malcolm Tucker
Rebecca Front
Nicola Murray
Chris Addison
Oliver Reeder
Joanna Scanlan
Terri Coverley
James Smith
Glenn Cullen
Miles Jupp
John Duggan

Melanie Hill
Julie Price
Lucinda Raikes
Angela Heaney

series 3, episode 4
(1st shown on Saturday, 14
November 2009 on BBC Two;
22:10–22:40) (29m 10s)

directed and devised by
Armando Iannucci
produced by
Adam Tandy
written by
Ian Martin
with
Jesse Armstrong
Simon Blackwell
Roger Drew
and
Will Smith
Sean Gray
Armando Iannucci
Tony Roche
additional material
the Cast
director of photography
Jamie Cairney
editor
Gary Dollner
production designer
Simon Rogers

©2009 BBC
Production Company
BBC

executive producers
Mark Freeland
Armando Iannucci
production executive
Sarah Hitchcock
production manager
Catherine Gosling
production coordinator
Lauriel Martin
location manager
Tom Howard
production runner
Louis Maunder
production accountant
Owain Jonkers
post-production
Framestore

1st assistant director
Charlie Leech
2nd assistant director
Jon Jennings
3rd assistant director
Daniel Castella
director's assistant
Will Smith
script supervisor
Elise Burgess
casting director
Sarah Crowe
script consultants
Martin Sixsmith
Kate Conway
research
Jackie Ramsamy
B camera operator
Greg Duffield
gaffer
Colin Thwaites
art director
Holly Berk
production buyer
Laura Marsh
costume designer
Ros Little
costume supervisor
Janine Marr
make-up designer
Judith Barkas
make-up artist
Nuala McArdle
sound recordist
Bob Newton
boom [operator]
Richard Pilcher
dubbing editor
Chris Maclean

cast
Peter Capaldi
Malcolm Tucker
Rebecca Front
Nicola Murray
Chris Addison
Oliver Reeder
Joanna Scanlan
Terri Coverley
James Smith
Glenn Cullen
Roger Allam
Peter Mannion
Vincent Franklin
Stewart Pearson

the thick of it

Olivia Poulet
Emma Messinger
Will Smith
Phil Smith
Simon Chandler
Permanent Secretary
Nick Sidi
head teacher

series 3, episode 5
(1st tx Saturday, 21 November 2009 on BBC Two; 22:20–22:50) (29m 13s)

directed and devised by
Armando Iannucci
produced by
Adam Tandy
written by
Roger Drew
and
Will Smith
Tony Roche
with
Simon Blackwell
Sean Gray
Armando Iannucci
additional dialogue
the Cast
director of photography
Jamie Cairney
editor
Gary Dollner
production designer
Simon Rogers

©2009 BBC
Production Company
BBC

executive producers
Mark Freeland
Armando Iannucci
production executive
Sarah Hitchcock
production manager
Francis Gilson
production coordinator
Lauriel Martin
location manager
Tom Howard
production runner
Louis Maunder
production accountant
Owain Jonkers

post-production
Framestore
1st assistant director
Jude Campbell
2nd assistant director
Jon Jennings
3rd assistant director
Daniel Castella
director's assistant
Ben Cotham
script supervisor
Elise Burgess
casting director
Sarah Crowe
script consultants
Martin Sixsmith
Kate Conway
B camera operator
Greg Duffield
gaffer
Colin Thwaites
art director
Holly Berk
props master
Craig Price
standby props
Paul Mitchell
production buyer
Laura Marsh
costume designer
Ros Little
costume supervisor
Janine Marr
costume assistant
Anita Ladd [Lad]
make-up designer
Judith Barkas
make-up artist
Nuala McArdle
sound recordist
Bob Newton
boom [operator]
Richard Pilcher
dubbing editor
Chris Maclean
thanks to
BBC Radio 5 Live

cast
Peter Capaldi
Malcolm Tucker
Rebecca Front
Nicola Murray
Chris Addison
Oliver Reeder

Joanna Scanlan
Terri Coverley
James Smith
Glenn Cullen
Roger Allam
Peter Mannion
Vincent Franklin
Stewart Pearson
Olivia Poulet
Emma Messinger
Will Smith
Phil Smith
Richard Bacon
himself
Sara Pascoe
Janice
Samantha Harrington
Sam
George Riley
sports presenter
Rachael Hodges
newsreader

series 3, episode 6
(1st tx Saturday, 28 November 2009 on BBC Two; 22:40–23:10) (29m 13s)

directed and devised by
Armando Iannucci
produced by
Adam Tandy
written by
Sean Gray
with
Simon Blackwell
Roger Drew
and
Will Smith
Armando Iannucci
Ian Martin
Tony Roche
additional material
the Cast
director of photography
Jamie Cairney
editor
Ant Boys
production designer
Simon Rogers

©2009 BBC
Production Company
BBC

bfi tv classics

executive producers
Mark Freeland
Armando Iannucci
production executive
Sarah Hitchcock
production manager
Catherine Gosling
production coordinator
Lauriel Martin
location manager
Tom Howard
unit manager
Patrick Burrows
production runner
Louis Maunder
production accountant
Owain Jonkers
post-production
Framestore
1st assistant director
Charlie Leech
2nd assistant director
Jon Jennings
3rd assistant director
Daniel Castella
director's assistant
Will Smith
script supervisor
Elise Burgess
casting director
Sarah Crowe
script consultants
Martin Sixsmith
Kate Conway
B camera operator
Greg Duffield
camera assistants
Gary Rogers
Tom Vincent
gaffer
Colin Thwaites
best boy
Richard Potter
art director
Holly Berk
props master
Craig Price
standby props
Paul Mitchell
production buyer
Laura Marsh
graphic artist
Barry Sexton
costume designer
Ros Little

costume supervisor
Janine Marr
costume assistant
Eleanor Spalding
make-up designer
Judith Barkas
make-up artist
Nuala McArdle
make-up assistant
Katy Richards
assistant editor
Sean Lyons
sound recordist
Bob Newton
boom [operator]
Richard Pilcher
B boom
Ben Coleman
dubbing editor
Chris Maclean

cast
Peter Capaldi
Malcolm Tucker
Rebecca Front
Nicola Murray
Chris Addison
Oliver Reeder
Joanna Scanlan
Terri Coverley
James Smith
Glenn Cullen
Justin Edwards
Ben Swain
Rufus Wright
Gavin Boyes
Robin Weaver
Bo Poraj
journalists

series 3, episode 7
(1st tx Saturday, 5 December 2009 on BBC Two; 22:30–23:00) (29m 10s)

directed and devised by
Armando Iannucci
produced by
Adam Tandy
written by
Simon Blackwell
Tony Roche
with
Jesse Armstrong
Roger Drew
and Will Smith
Sean Gray
Armando Iannucci
Ian Martin
additional material
the Cast
director of photography
Jamie Cairney
editors
Ant Boys
Gary Dollner
production designer
Simon Rogers

©2009 BBC
Production Company
BBC

executive producers
Mark Freeland
Armando Iannucci
production executive
Sarah Hitchcock
production manager
Francis Gilson
production coordinator
Lauriel Martin
location manager
Tom Howard
unit manager
Patrick Burrows
production runner
Louis Maunder
production accountant
Owain Jonkers
post-production
Framestore
1st assistant director
Jude Campbell
2nd assistant director
Jon Jennings
3rd assistant director
Daniel Castella
director's assistant
Ben Cottam
script supervisor
Elise Burgess
casting director
Sarah Crowe
script consultants
Martin Sixsmith
Kate Conway
B camera operator
Greg Duffield

the thick of it

camera assistants
Gary Rogers
Tom Vincent
gaffer
Colin Thwaites
best boy
Richard Potter
art director
Holly Berk
props master
Craig Price
standby props
Paul Mitchell
production buyer
Laura Marsh
graphic artist
Barry Sexton
costume designer
Ros Little
costume supervisor
Janine Marr
costume assistant
Anita Ladd [Lad]
make-up designer
Judith Barkas
make-up artist
Nuala McArdle
colourist
Simon Bourne
VFX editor
Alix Ludlam
VFX producer
Magdalena Przézdziecka
sound recordist
Bob Newton
boom [operator]
Richard Pilcher
B boom
Ben Coleman
dubbing mixer
Chris Maclean
dubbing editor
Matt Brace

cast
Peter Capaldi
Malcolm Tucker
Rebecca Front
Nicola Murray
Chris Addison
Oliver Reeder
Joanna Scanlan
Terri Coverley
James Smith
Glenn Cullen
Peter Sullivan
Geoffrey
Zoë Telford
Marianne Swift
David Haig
Steve Fleming
Alex Macqueen
Lord Nicholson
Samantha Harrington
Sam

series 3, episode 8
(1st tx Saturday, 12 December 2009 on BBC Two; 22:10–22:40) (29m 5s)

directed and devised by
Armando Iannucci
produced by
Adam Tandy
written by
Jesse Armstrong
Simon Blackwell
with
Roger Drew
and
Will Smith
Sean Gray
Armando Iannucci
Ian Martin
Tony Roche
additional material
the Cast
director of photography
Jamie Cairney
editors
Gary Dollner
Ant Boys
production designer
Simon Rogers

©2009 BBC
Production Company
BBC

executive producers
Mark Freeland
Armando Iannucci
production executive
Sarah Hitchcock
production manager
Francis Gilson
production coordinator
Lauriel Martin
location manager
Tom Howard
unit manager
Patrick Burrows
production runner
Louis Maunder
production accountant
Owain Jonkers
post-production
Framestore
1st assistant director
Jude Campbell
2nd assistant director
Jon Jennings
3rd assistant director
Daniel Castella
director's assistant
Ben Cottam
script supervisor
Elise Burgess
script secretary
Angharad Parry
casting director
Sarah Crowe
script consultants
Martin Sixsmith
Kate Conway
B camera operator
Greg Duffield
camera assistants
Gary Rogers
Tom Vincent
gaffer
Colin Thwaites
best boy
Richard Potter
art director
Holly Berk
props master
Craig Price
standby props
Paul Mitchell
production buyer
Laura Marsh
graphic artist
Barry Sexton
costume designer
Ros Little
costume supervisor
Janine Marr
costume assistant
Anita Ladd [Lad]
make-up designer
Judith Barkas
make-up artist
Nuala McArdle
colourist
Simon Bourne

bfi tv classics

VFX editor
Will Yarrow
VFX producer
Magdalena Przézdziecka
sound recordist
Bob Newton
boom [operator]
Richard Pilcher
B boom
Ben Coleman
dubbing mixer
Chris Maclean
dubbing editor
Matt Brace
archive research
Jonathan Harvey

cast
Peter Capaldi
Malcolm Tucker
Rebecca Front
Nicola Murray
Chris Addison
Oliver Reeder
Joanna Scanlan
Terri Coverley
James Smith
Glenn Cullen
David Haig
Steve Fleming
Alex Macqueen
Lord Nicholson
Samantha Harrington
Sam
Roger Allam
Peter Mannion
Vincent Franklin
Stewart Pearson
Olivia Poulet
Emma Messinger
Will Smith
Phil Smith
Tom Hollander
Cal Richards
Struan Rodger
Pat
Susy Kane
BBC producer

series 4, episode 1
(1st tx Saturday, 8 September 2012 on BBC One;
21:45–22:15) (28m 55s)

directed by
Natalie Bailey

produced and devised by
Armando Iannucci
produced by
Adam Tandy
written by
Will Smith
with
Simon Blackwell
Sean Gray
Ian Martin
David Quantick
Tony Roche
additional material
Roger Drew
Dan Gaster
the Cast
director of photography
Jamie Cairney
editor
Ant Boys
production designer
Simon Rogers

©2012 BBC
Production Companies
a BBC Productions/Hulu co-production

executive producer for Hulu
Andy Forssell
executive producer for BBC
Mark Freeland
production executive
Sarah Hitchcock
production manager
Maria Cooper
production coordinator
Laura Park
location manager
Alex Cox
unit manager
Eleanor Downey
floor runner
Tilly Gerrard-Bannister
production accountant
Josie Kelly
1st assistant director
Chris May
2nd assistant director
Nikki Molloy
3rd assistant director
Sam Smith
script supervisor
Angelica Pressello
script coordinator
Annika Magnberg

script assistant
Laura Shaw
casting director
Sarah Crowe
script consultant
Kate Conway
new research
Ben Spiteri
A camera operator
Nick Martin
camera assistants
Tom Vincent
Jess Carrivick
gaffer
Colin Thwaites
best boy
Peter Gilmour
art director
Antony Cartlidge
props master
Laurence Archer
standby props
Dean Brandon
Kevin Scarrott
Peter J. Simons
production buyer
Amanda George
props storeman
Mark Bevan
costume designer
Jackie Vernon
costume supervisor
Janine Marr
costume assistant
Tom Reeve
make-up designer
Judith Barkas
make-up supervisor
Jayne Buxton
make-up artist
Kate Morgan
assistant editor
Jo Walker
post-production supervisor
Vanessa Lees
post-production
Framestore
sound recordist
Bob Newton
boom
Richard Pilcher
A boom
David Turnbull
dubbing mixer
Chris Maclean

the thick of it

cast
Roger Allam
Peter Mannion
Will Smith
Phil Smith
Joanna Scanlan
Terri Coverley
Ben Willbond
Adam Kenyon
Geoffrey Streatfeild
Fergus Williams
James Smith
Glenn Cullen
Vincent Franklin
Stewart Pearson
Olivia Poulet
Emma Messinger
Hamza Jeetooa
Raj
Jessica Henwick
Charlotte
Dave Florez
teacher
Tom Andrews
Adam Tandy
Gareth Tunley
Martha Cope
Manjinder Virk
Dan Mersh
journalists

series 4, episode 2
(1st tx Saturday, 15
September 2012 on BBC One;
21:55–22:25) (28m 11s)

directed by
Billy Sneddon
produced and devised by
Armando Iannucci
produced by
Adam Tandy
written by
Simon Blackwell
with
Roger Drew
Dan Gaster
Sean Gray
Ian Martin
additional material
Georgia Pritchett
Tony Roche
Will Smith
the Cast

directors of photography
Jamie Cairney
Nick Martin
editor
Ant Boys
production designer
Simon Rogers

©2012 BBC
Production Companies
a BBC Productions/Hulu
co-production

executive producer for Hulu
Andy Forssell
executive producer for BBC
Mark Freeland
production executive
Sarah Hitchcock
production manager
Maria Cooper
production coordinator
Laura Park
location manager
Alex Cox
unit manager
Eleanor Downey
floor runner
Tilly Gerrard-Bannister
production accountant
Josie Kelly
1st assistant director
Chris May
2nd assistant director
Nikki Molloy
3rd assistant director
Sam Smith
script supervisor
Angelica Pressello
script coordinator
Annika Magnberg
script assistant
Laura Shaw
casting director
Sarah Crowe
artists' contracts
Mike Bickerdike
Michelle Sally
new research
Ben Spiteri
B camera operator
Adrian Marciante
camera assistants
Tom Vincent
Jess Carrivick

gaffer
Colin Thwaites
best boy
Peter Gilmour
art director
Antony Cartlidge
props master
Laurence Archer
standby props
Dean Brandon
Kevin Scarrott
Peter J. Simons
production buyer
Amanda George
props storeman
Mark Bevan
costume designer
Jackie Vernon
costume supervisor
Janine Marr
costume assistant
Tom Reeve
make-up designer
Judith Barkas
make-up artist
Kate Morgan
assistant editor
Jo Walker
post-production supervisor
Vanessa Lees
post-production
Framestore
sound recordist
Bob Newton
boom
Richard Pilcher
B boom
David Turnbull
dubbing mixer
Chris Maclean

cast
Peter Capaldi
Malcolm Tucker
Justin Edwards
Ben Swain
Rebecca Front
Nicola Murray
Rebecca Gethings
Helen Hatley
Chris Addison
Oliver Reeder
Tony Gardner
Dan Miller

121

Samantha Harrington
Sam
Rob Edwards
Geoff Holhurst
Michael Colgan
Mr Chop
Chetna Pandya
Gareth Tunley
journalists

series 4, episode 3
(1st tx Saturday, 22
September 2012 on BBC Two;
21:55–22:25) (28m 32s)

directed by
Natalie Bailey
produced and devised by
Armando Iannucci
produced by
Adam Tandy
written by
Will Smith
with
Simon Blackwell
Sean Gray
Ian Martin
David Quantick
Tony Roche
additional material
Roger Drew
Dan Gaster
the Cast
directors of photography
Jamie Cairney
Nick Martin
editor
Gary Dollner
production designer
Simon Rogers

©2012 BBC
Production Companies
a BBC Productions/Hulu
co-production

executive producer for Hulu
Andy Forssell
executive producer for BBC
Mark Freeland
production executive
Sarah Hitchcock
production manager
Maria Cooper
production coordinator
Laura Park

location manager
Alex Cox
unit manager
Eleanor Downey
floor runner
Tilly Gerrard-Bannister
production accountant
Josie Kelly
1st assistant director
Chris May
2nd assistant director
Nikki Molloy
3rd assistant director
Sam Smith
script supervisor
Angelica Pressello
script coordinator
Annika Magnberg
script assistant
Laura Shaw
casting director
Sarah Crowe
artists' contracts
Mike Bickerdike
Michelle Sally
new research
Ben Spiteri
B camera operator
Adrian Marciante
camera assistants
Tom Vincent
Jess Carrivick
gaffer
Colin Thwaites
best boy
Peter Gilmour
art director
Antony Cartlidge
props master
Laurence Archer
standby props
Dean Brandon
Kevin Scarrott
Peter J. Simons
production buyer
Amanda George
props storeman
Mark Bevan
costume designer
Jackie Vernon
costume supervisor
Janine Marr
costume assistant
Tom Reeve
make-up designer
Judith Barkas

make-up supervisor
Jayne Buxton
make-up artist
Kate Morgan
assistant editor
Jo Walker
post-production supervisor
Vanessa Lees
post-production
Framestore
sound recordist
Bob Newton
boom
Richard Pilcher
B boom
David Turnbull
dubbing mixer
Chris Maclean

cast
Roger Allam
Peter Mannion
Olivia Poulet
Emma Messinger
Vincent Franklin
Stewart Pearson
Will Smith
Phil Smith
Ben Willbond
Adam Kenyon
Geoffrey Streatfeild
Fergus Williams
Joanna Scanlan
Terri Coverley
Sylvestra Le Touzel
Mary Drake
Emily Bevan
Tara Strachan
Teresa Churcher
receptionist
Tom Andrews
Adam Tandy
Gareth Tunley
journalists

series 4, episode 4
(1st tx Saturday, 29
September 2012 on BBC Two;
21:45–22:15) (29m 3s)

directed by
Becky Martin
produced and devised by
Armando Iannucci
produced by
Adam Tandy

the thick of it

written by
Sean Gray
with
Simon Blackwell
Tony Roche
additional material
Roger Drew
Ian Martin
Will Smith
the Cast
director of photography
Jamie Cairney
editor
Ant Boys
production designer
Simon Rogers

©2012 BBC
Production Companies
a BBC Productions/Hulu co-production

executive producer for Hulu
Andy Forssell
executive producer for BBC
Mark Freeland
production executive
Sarah Hitchcock
production manager
Maria Cooper
production coordinator
Laura Park
location manager
Alex Cox
unit manager
Eleanor Downey
floor runner
Tilly Gerrard-Bannister
production accountant
Josie Kelly
1st assistant director
Natalie Segal
2nd assistant director
Nikki Molloy
3rd assistant director
Russell Dewulff-Booth
script supervisor
Angelica Pressello
script coordinator
Annika Magnberg
script assistant
Laura Shaw
casting director
Sarah Crowe
new research
Ben Spiteri

A camera operator
Nick Martin
camera assistants
Tom Vincent
Jess Carrivick
gaffer
Colin Thwaites
best boy
Peter Gilmour
Art Director
Antony Cartlidge
props master
Laurence Archer
standby props
Dean Brandon
Kevin Scarrott
Peter J. Simons
production buyer
Amanda George
props storeman
Mark Bevan
costume designer
Jackie Vernon
costume supervisor
Anita Lad
costume assistant
Janine Marr
make-up designer
Judith Barkas
make-up artist
Kate Morgan
assistant editor
Jo Walker
post-production supervisor
Vanessa Lees
post-production
Framestore
colourists
Simon Bourne
Edwin Metternich
VFX editors
Matt Clarke
Mark Chapman
VFX producer
Andrew McLintock
sound recordist
Bob Newton
boom
Richard Pilcher
B boom
David Turnbull
dubbing mixer
Chris Maclean
dubbing editor
Matthew Brace

assistant dubbing editor
Rick Morris
sound assistant
Adam Kidd

cast
Peter Capaldi
Malcolm Tucker
Chris Addison
Oliver Reeder
Rebecca Front
Nicola Murray
Rebecca Gethings
Helen Hatley
James Smith
Glenn Cullen
Tony Gardner
Dan Miller
Zahra Ahmadi
nurse
Miles Jupp
John Duggan
Lucy Briers
Cathy Hastings
Justin Edwards
Ben Swain

series 4, episode 5
(1st tx Saturday, 13 October 2012 on BBC Two; 21:30–22:00) (28m 40s)

directed by
Chris Addison
produced and devised by
Armando Iannucci
produced by
Adam Tandy
written by
Roger Drew
with
Sean Gray
additional material
Simon Blackwell
Rob Colley
Dan Gaster
Ian Martin
David Quantick
Tony Roche
Will Smith
the Cast
directors of photography
Jamie Cairney
Nick Martin
editor
Gary Dollner

bfi tv classics

production designer
Simon Rogers

©2012 BBC
Production Companies
a BBC Productions/Hulu
co-production

executive producer for Hulu
Andy Forssell
executive producer for BBC
Mark Freeland
production executive
Sarah Hitchcock
production manager
Maria Cooper
production coordinator
Laura Park
location manager
Alex Cox
unit manager
Eleanor Downey
floor runner
Tilly Gerrard-Bannister
production accountant
Josie Kelly
1st assistant director
Chris May
2nd assistant director
Nikki Molloy
3rd assistant director
Sam Smith
script supervisor
Angelica Pressello
script coordinator
Annika Magnberg
script assistant
Laura Shaw
casting director
Sarah Crowe
new research
Ben Spiteri
B camera operator
Adrian Marciante
camera assistants
Tom Vincent
Jess Carrivick
gaffer
Colin Thwaites
best boy
Peter Gilmour
art director
Antony Cartlidge
props master
Laurence Archer

standby props
Dean Brandon
Kevin Scarrott
Peter J. Simons
production buyer
Amanda George
props storeman
Mark Bevan
costume designer
Jackie Vernon
costume supervisor
Janine Marr
costume assistant
Tom Reeve
make-up designer
Judith Barkas
make-up artist
Kate Morgan
assistant editor
Jo Walker
post-production supervisor
Vanessa Lees
post-production
Framestore
sound recordist
Bob Newton
boom
Richard Pilcher
B boom
David Turnbull
dubbing mixer
Chris Maclean

cast
Rebecca Front
Nicola Murray
Rebecca Gethings
Helen Hatley
Will Smith
Phil Smith
Roger Allam
Peter Mannion
Olivia Poulet
Emma Messinger
Vincent Franklin
Stewart Pearson
Geoffrey Streatfeild
Fergus Williams
Ben Willbond
Adam Kenyon
Joanna Scanlan
Terri Coverley
Michael Colgan
Mr Chop

James Smith
Glenn Cullen
Polly Kemp
Robyn Murdoch
Joe Cole
Jack
Mandeep Dhillon
Rohinka
Peter Capaldi
Malcolm Tucker
Tony Gardner
Dan Miller
Chris Addison
Oliver Reeder
Samantha Harrington
Sam

series 4, episode 6
(1st tx Saturday, 20 October 2012 on BBC Two;
21:45–22:45) (59m 10s)

directed and devised by
Armando Iannucci
produced by
Adam Tandy
written by
Simon Blackwell
Roger Drew
Dan Gaster
Sean Gray
Ian Martin
Georgia Pritchett
David Quantick
Tony Roche
Will Smith
additional material
the Cast
director of photography
Jamie Cairney
editors
Gary Dollner
Robin Hill
Billy Sneddon
production designer
Simon Rogers

©2012 BBC
Production Companies
a BBC Productions/Hulu
co-production

executive producer for Hulu
Andy Forssell

the thick of it

executive producer for BBC
Mark Freeland
production executive
Sarah Hitchcock
production manager
Maria Cooper
production coordinator
Laura Park
location manager
Alex Cox
unit manager
Eleanor Downey
floor runner
Tilly Gerrard-Bannister
production accountant
Josie Kelly
1st assistant director
Chris May
2nd assistant director
Nikki Molloy
3rd assistant directors
Sam Smith
Izzy Shearman
script supervisor
Angelica Pressello
script coordinator
Annika Magnberg
script assistant
Laura Shaw
casting director
Sarah Crowe
A camera operator
Nick Martin
camera assistants
Tom Vincent
Jess Carrivick
gaffer
Colin Thwaites
best boy
Peter Gilmour
art director
Antony Cartlidge
props master
Laurence Archer
standby props
Dean Brandon
Jack Berk
Peter J. Simons
production buyer
Amanda George
props storeman
Mark Bevan
costume designer
Jackie Vernon

costume supervisor
Janine Marr
costume assistant
Tom Reeve
make-up designer
Judith Barkas
make-up artist
Kate Morgan
assistant editor
Jo Walker
post-production supervisor
Vanessa Lees
post-production
Framestore
sound recordist
Bob Newton
boom
Richard Pilcher
B boom
David Turnbull
dubbing mixer
Chris Maclean

cast
William Hoyland
Lord Goolding
Tobias Menzies
Simon Weir
Priyanga Burford
Baroness Sureka
Michael Maloney
Matthew Hodge
Vincent Franklin
Stewart Pearson
Peter Capaldi
Malcolm Tucker
Geoffrey Streatfeild
Fergus Williams
Roger Allan
Peter Mannion
Olivia Poulet
Emma Messinger
Will Smith
Phil Smith
Ben Willbond
Adam Kenyon
Joanna Scanlan
Terri Coverley
Rebecca Front
Nicola Murray
Polly Kemp
Robyn Murdoch
Chris Addison
Oliver Reeder

James Smith
Glenn Cullen

series 4, episode 7
(1st tx Saturday, 27 October
2012 on BBC Two;
21:30–22:00) (28m 42s)

directed by
Tony Roche
produced and devised by
Armando Iannucci
produced by
Adam Tandy
written by
Tony Roche
with
Simon Blackwell
Sean Gray
Ian Martin
Will Smith
additional material
the Cast
director of photography
Jamie Cairney
editor
Gary Dollner
production designer
Simon Rogers

©2012 BBC
Production Companies
a BBC Productions/Hulu
co-production

executive producer for Hulu
Andy Forssell
executive producer for BBC
Mark Freeland
production executive
Sarah Hitchcock
production manager
Maria Cooper
production coordinator
Laura Park
location manager
Alex Cox
unit manager
Eleanor Downey
floor runner
Tilly Gerrard-Bannister
production accountant
Josie Kelly
1st assistant director
Chris May

bfi tv classics

2nd assistant director
Nikki Molloy
3rd assistant directors
Sam Smith
Izzy Shearman
script supervisor
Angelica Pressello
script coordinator
Annika Magnberg
script assistant
Laura Shaw
casting director
Sarah Crowe
A camera operator
Nick Martin
camera assistants
Tom Vincent
Jess Carrivick
gaffer
Colin Thwaites
best boy
Peter Gilmour
art director
Antony Cartlidge
props master
Laurence Archer
standby props
Dean Brandon
Jack Berk
Peter J. Simons
production buyer
Amanda George
props storeman
Mark Bevan
costume designer
Jackie Vernon

costume supervisor
Janine Marr
costume assistant
Tom Reeve
make-up designer
Judith Barkas
make-up artist
Kate Morgan
assistant editor
Jo Walker
post-production supervisor
Vanessa Lees
post-production
Framestore
sound recordist
Bob Newton
boom
Richard Pilcher
B boom
David Turnbull
dubbing mixer
Chris Maclean

cast
Joanna Scanlan
Terri Coverley
Olivia Poulet
Emma Messinger
Will Smith
Phil Smith
Geoffrey Streatfeild
Fergus Williams
Ben Willbond
Adam Kenyon
James Smith
Glenn Cullen

Roger Allan
Peter Mannion
Chris Addison
Oliver Reeder
Tony Gardner
Dan Miller
Peter Capaldi
Malcolm Tucker
Samantha Harrington
Sam
Vincent Franklin
Stewart Pearson
Sylvestra Le Touzel
Mary Drake
Rebecca Front
Nicola Murray
Rebecca Gethings
Helen Hatley
Michael Colgan
Declan
Colin Mace
desk sergeant
Simon Kunz
Greg Fraser
Michael Gould
superintendent
Adam G. Goodwin
prisoner
Adam Stevens
police officer
Dan Mersh
journalist

Credits compiled by Julian Grainger

Index

A
Absolutely Fabulous 95
Addison, Chris 19, 96
Adonis, Lord (Andrew) 16
Airport 36
Alan Partridge: Alpha Papa 95
Ali G 7
alignment 34–5
Allam, Roger 16
Are You Being Served? 95
Armstrong, Jesse 96
authenticity, codes of 37

B
Baynham, Peter 105n
BBC 67
BBC Four 1
BBC Radio 4 5, 55
BBC Radio 5 20
BBC Radio 5 Live 92
BBC Two 1
Bentinck, Tim 30
The Big Breakfast 20
Blackwell, Simon 96
Blair, Tony 7–8, 17, 20
Blunkett, David 18
Bowen, Jim 20
Bowie, David, 'Changes' 8
British Academy of Film and Television Arts 1
'British business bank' 9
Brown, Gordon 20, 22
Brown, Tom 29
Budget 11
Burford, Priyanka 43
Byrne, Michael 62

C
Cable, Vince 9
Cameron, David 7–8, 13, 15
Campbell, Alastair 8, 12, 16–22
Campbell, Sir Menzies 6–7
Capaldi, Peter 12, 20, 23, 33, *39*, 60, 69, 96
Catholicism 22
Citizen Kane 15–16, 23
Clarke, Kenneth 16
Cold Feet 95
Conservative Party 20, 29
Coogan, Steve 5, 37, 98, 105n
Coulson, Andy 23
The Cruise 36

D
Dad's Army 95
Daily Mail 32
Daily Mirror 42
Davis, Lucy 78
The Day Today 5–7, 9, 105n
Dhillon, Mandeep 73
docusoaps 36–7
Drew, Roger 8, 96
Driving School 36

E
EastEnders 20
Eddington, Paul 62
Edwards, Justin 10
ER 36

Evans, Suzanne 7–8
Evening Standard 55

F
Facebook 3, 93
Fawlty Towers 95
Fielding, Steven 103–4
Fiske, John, and John Hartley, *Reading Television* 1
Freeman, Martin 78
Friends 76–7, 78–80, 89
Front, Rebecca 5, 12, 105n

G
Gandolfini, James 99
Gardner, Tony 42
Gaza 98
Gervais, Ricky 78
Gethings, Rebecca 87
GQ 20
Gray, Sean 9–13, 96
Groundhog Day 14
the *Guardian* 20, 69–70

H
Haig, David 16
Hale, Tony 100
Harman, Harriet 17, 18
Harrington, Samantha 84
Hawthorne, Nigel 62–3
Hearst, William Randolph 15–16
Henry VIII, King 22
Higgins, Paul 10
Hilton, Steve 16

Him & Her 36
Hoddinott, Diana 89
Hollander, Tom 98
Hollywood 2, 23
House of Cards:
　(UK version) 27–30, *28*
　(US version) 101, 105n
House of Commons 10–13
Hoyland, William 8
Hyman, Peter 17

I
Iannucci, Armando 5, 7–8, 9, 16, 37, 62, 95, 98, 103–4
I'm Alan Partridge 37
In the Loop 1, 16–17, 95–9, 102–4
In the Loop, characters:
　Karen Clark 98–9
　Dan 97
　Simon Foster 98–9
　Jamie McDonald 97, 102
　General Miller 99
　Judy Molloy 96
　Michael Rodgers 102
　Toby 96–7
　Malcolm Tucker 16, 97, 102, 104
The Inbetweeners Movie 95
Ineson, Ralph 78
Ingham, Bernard 22
Iraq, invasion of 17, 21, 98, 102

J
Jolie, Angelina 3
Jones, Nicholas 22

K
Kemp, Polly 83
Kennedy, Mimi 98

L
Labour Party 20
　as New Labour 16, 21–2
Langham, Chris 38
The League of Gentlemen's Apocalypse 95
Leveson Inquiry 41
Liberal Democrat party 6, 9, 20
Linehan, Graham 105n
London Oratory school 17
Louis-Dreyfus, Julia 99
Lury, Karen 76

M
McBride, Damian 22
McKee, Gina 96
McPherson, Fiona 13
Macqueen, Alex 16
Mandelson, Peter 16, 21–2
Martin, Ian 96
Mathews, Arthur 105n
May, James 20
Men Behaving Badly 95
Menzies, Tobias 68
Miliband, Ed 11–13
Millar, Fiona 18–19
Mills, Brett 105n
miners' strike 22
Miramax 23
Moore, Martin 22
Morris, Chris 5, 6
Mrs Brown's Boys D'Movie 95
Mulvey, Laura 15–16, 23

N
New York 77
Newsnight 10, *11*, 15, 20
Northampton 98

O
Observer 4–5, 9, 13–14
The Office 36, 37, 77–81, *79*
'omnishambles' 11–13
On the Buses 95
On the Hour 5
Oxford English Dictionary 13

P
Paxman, Jeremy 6, 10, 20–81
Perkins, V. F. 35
Pitt, Brad 3
Poulet, Olivia 45
Prime Minister's Questions 10–12
Pritchett, Georgia 96
Public Administration Select Committee, 'Special Advisers in the Thick of It' 14

Q
Quantick, David 96
Question Time 7–8, 67

R
Raikes, Lucinda 81
Ramis, Harold 14
reality television 36–7
Richards, Paul, *Be Your Own Spin Doctor* 21
Richardson, Ian 26, 27, *28*
Roche, Tony 96
Roger and Val Have Just Got In 36
Royal Television Society 1
The Royle Family 35–6, 37

S

Scanlan, Joanna 30
Schneider, David 5, 105n
Shakespeare, William,
  Richard III 29
Simons, Timothy 99
sitcoms 35–6, 76–80
Sky News 20, 87, 88
Smith, Chloe 10
Smith, James 38, 102
Smith, Murray 34
Smith, Will 8, 45, 96, 97
Spaced 95
Spacey, Kevin 26
Star Wars 20
Streatfeild, Geoffrey 42
synthesis 35

T

That Peter Kay Thing 36
Thatcher, Margaret 20, 22, 27–30
The Thick of It, characters:
  Hugh Abbot 38, 40, 55–8, 80, 81–3, 85–6, 88, 90–1
  Terri Coverley 30–1, 40, 44, 55, 59–61, 65, 67, 81, 83, 91
  Glenn Cullen 38, 40, 45, 55, 56, 60, 80, 81, 86
  John Duggan 87
  Steve Fleming 16, 59, 83–4, 88, 92
  Helen Hatley 87
  Angela Heaney 81–3
  Adam Kenyon 44, 72–3
  Cliff Lawton 30–4, 38, 40, 46
  Jamie McDonald 10, 97, 102
  Peter Mannion 16, 44, 72, 85, 92
  Emma Messinger 45, 91–2
  Dan Miller 42, 43, 45, 81
  Nicola Murray 12, 17–18, 23, 42, 43, 44, 58–60, 65–7, 72, 84, 86–90, 92
  Julius Nicholson 16, 38, 40, 81, 84
  Stewart Pearson 16, 41, 44–5, 85
  Ollie Reeder 19, 38, 40, 45–6, 55, 60, 68–9, 80, 87, 91–2, 96–7
  Robyn 83, 86
  Rohinka 73
  Sam 84
  Phil Smith 45, 91–2, 97
  Baroness Sureka 43
  Ben Swain 10, 44, 60, 87
  Mr Tickell 44
  Malcolm Tucker 12, 16–23, 31–5, 38–46, 55–62, 65–73, 81–4, 87–8, 92–3, 97, 102, 104
  Simon Weir 68
  Fergus Williams 42, 44, 72–3
This Life 36
Thomas, Deborah 75, 80
Time Trumpet 8–9
Tumblr 3, *3*
Twitter 93

U

UKIP (United Kingdom Independence Party) 7

V

Veep 1, 95–7, 99–104, *100*

W

Washington, DC 98
  UN building 102
Weinstein, Harvey 23
Welles, Orson 15
The West Wing 101
White, Michael 103
Willbond, Ben 44
Wollaston, Sam 69–70
Wood, Robin, *Hitchcock's Films* 2
World at One 55

Y

Yes, Minister 62, 71
Yes, Prime Minister 62–5, 67, 71, 89, *90*, 91
YouGov poll 12
The Young Ones 95
YouTube 3, 7–8

bfi tv classics

Also Published:

The Beiderbecke Affair
William Gallagher
Bleak House
Christine Geraghty
Buffy the Vampire Slayer
Anne Billson
Cathy Come Home
Stephen Lacey
Civilisation
Jonathan Conlin
Cracker
Mark Duguid
CSI: Crime Scene Investigation
Steven Cohan
Deadwood
Jason Jacobs
Doctor Who
Kim Newman
Edge of Darkness
John Caughie
Law and Order
Charlotte Brunsdon

The League of Gentlemen
Leon Hunt

The Likely Lads
Phil Wickham
The Office
Ben Walters
Our Friends in the North
Michael Eaton
Prime Suspect
Deborah Jermyn
Queer as Folk
Glyn Davis
Seinfeld
Nicholas Mirzoeff
Seven Up
Stella Bruzzi
The Singing Detective
Glen Creeber
Star Trek
Ina Rae Hark
The World at War
Taylor Downing